Creative  ojects

Sugarcraft
Creations

Publisher's Note: Raw or semi-cooked eggs should not be consumed by babies, toddlers, pregnant or breastfeeding women, the elderly or those suffering from a chronic illness.

Publisher & Creative Director: Nick Wells
Senior Project Editor: Catherine Taylor
Picture Research: Esme Chapman and Catherine Taylor
Copy Editor: Kathy Steer
Art Director: Mike Spender
Layout Design: Jane Ashley
Digital Design & Production: Chris Herbert

Special thanks to Ann Nicol, Frances Bodiam and the suppliers below.

For cake-decorating supplies, colours and shimmers by mail order: **Squires Kitchen**, Squires Group, Squires House, 3 Waverley Lane, Farnham, Surrey, GU9 8BB. Tel: 0845 617 1801 www.squires-shop.com

Discover 1000s more inspiring baking and decorating ideas at **lakeland.co.uk**. For embossing tools, moulds, sugarcraft supplies and bakeware by mail order: **Lakeland**, Alexandria Buildings, Windermere, Cumbria, LA23 1BQ. Tel: 01539 488 100.

An extensive range of sugarcraft supplies are available from **cakedecoratingstore.co.uk**.

This is a **FLAME TREE** Book

FLAME TREE PUBLISHING
Crabtree Hall, Crabtree Lane
Fulham, London SW6 6TY
United Kingdom
www.flametreepublishing.com

First published 2014

Copyright © 2014 Flame Tree Publishing Ltd

14 16 18 17 15
1 3 5 4 2

ISBN: 978-1-78361-302-1

A copy of the CIP data for this book is available from the British Library.

Printed in Singapore

Image credits: Courtesy **Shutterstock.com** and the following: Goldnetz 10; Tom Mc Nemar 12; Ruth Black 13b & 74; Mshev 19; Dragon Images 34b; Olga Kovalenko 35t; Kosoff 36; Dustin Dennis 38b; lapas77 39 & 40t; Agnes Kantaruk 43; Steve Buckley 44; Lestertair 49; denio109 51t; Szasz-Fabian Jozsef 51b; Viktor1 52; ARENA Creative 53; Surkov Vladmir 60; infinity21 62; pp09 64; Maria Sbytova 66; Igor Link 68; staras 70; Agnes Kantaruk 72; val lawless 80; MNStudio 84; Giordano Alta 92; NDT 94; svry 96; Ozgur Coskun 98 & 118; Oleg – F 100; ljansempoi 106; Irina Schmidt 108 & 154; Prezoom.nl 110; gosphotodesign 112; krsmanovic 114; Dulce Rubia 120; Pete Pahham 122 & 198; Nickola_Che 124; Martin Nemec 134; Christopher Elwell 142 & 206; anki21 146; Jeanie333 156; Superlime 158 & 168 & 182 & 220 & 246; Koraysa 180; Andrey Starostin 186; Lesya Dolyuk 194; FomaA 200; Robyn Mackenzie 202; Olga Lyubkina 214; Glenn Young 218. Courtesy **Cakedecoratingstore.co.uk:** 11 & 13t & 34t & 35b & 36b & 37t & 37m & 37b & 38m & 40b. © **Flame Tree Publishing Ltd:** 12b, 15, 17, 27, 32, 41, 42, 44t, 45b, 46, 47, 48t, 50c, 50b, 52t, 53b. © **iStock.com** and the following: lillisphotography 58; AnisimovaAlesya 126; SchulteProductions 128; lanych 130; RBOZUK 138 & 166; MarcoGovel 148; penguenstok 162; scorpion56 164; boggy22 196; bycostello photography 208; ihorga 210 & 212; Sezer Alcinkaya 242; dhoffmanimages 244. Courtesy **Getty Images** and the following: Kathryn Harris/4Goodnesscake 76; Alexandra Gablewski 78; Ngoc Minh Ngo 82; Luzia Ellert 140; Jasmine Burgess 184; altrendo travel 188; Westend61 190; susan.k. 248.

Creative and Practical Projects

Sugarcraft Creations

**FLAME TREE
PUBLISHING**

Contents

Introduction

Cake decorating has become an extremely popular hobby over the last few years; now the enthusiastic amateur baker can create beautiful decorated cakes and celebration cakes that look really professional. As well as decorative patterns and icings, they can be topped off with sugarcraft models. This is the ideal book to help you if you want to take your cake-decorating projects that little bit further by making models and themed fantasy creations. With lots of new ideas, this book shows you how to make your sugarcraft creations look really special.

If you have mastered the basics of cake decorating, you will probably want to extend your skills a little further. Contemporary sugarcraft uses all sorts of techniques to create stunning results, with lots of new skills being developed all the time. *Sugarcraft Creations* will show you how to use these new methods, such as embossing and using moulds, to produce quick and easy results that will amaze your guests.

Each chapter is filled with beautifully photographed projects to inspire you. In the first section, we help you cover the essentials needed for creating works in sugarcraft, including sugarcraft ingredients and an equipment section which shows some of the fantastic selection of cake-decorating equipment now available – for example, the new ranges of special moulds on sale now will help you to achieve striking results quickly and easily; we also remind you of the recipes for the basic icings and coverings and explain how to use the different types of modelling pastes. At the back of the book, you will find templates of designs to copy.

This book covers a range of thematic interests – you will find sugarpaste transformed into many wonderful shapes and varied forms. Look out for your favourite critters in the Animal Friends chapter. Some are ideal for younger children's birthdays and parties – cakes featuring bears, a cute kitty, a Dalmatian or a penguin are sure to be popular. The People chapter shows you how to make ever-popular figures such as a princess or a footballer, and the angel or Santa will help you celebrate the festive season. The Seasonal & Celebration chapter will show you how to create special models for baby showers and christenings with cute booties or a baby carriage. For wedding celebrations, you will love the Scruffy Wedding Bears or a sweet wedding couple. Special projects for your friends and family with hobbies include knitting- or camping-themed models, or for those who just love handbags and shoes, we have the ideal sugarcraft fashion creations.

Sugarcraft has come a long way over the past few years; now there are even a huge variety of classes available and you will also find blogs and websites devoted to the subject. When you begin in sugarcraft you will learn by copying designs, but, as your confidence grows, you will find that you will want to create your own ideas and make your projects more adventurous. *Sugarcraft Creations* will inspire you to give your decorated cakes that perfect finish and that little extra special touch to make them unique.

Happy decorating, **Ann Nicol**

Introduction

Sugarcraft
Basics

We're assuming you've already baked your cake, and possibly iced it too, but that you don't know everything you need to know regarding decoration and sugarcraft techniques. So have a read of this section before you get stuck into modelling your creations. Here we cover key decorating ingredients and icing recipes, from buttercream to sugarpaste; useful equipment, including moulds, cutters and tools; and essential techniques, such as making basic flowers.

Decorating Ingredients

There are a multitude of ingredients you can use to decorate your creations. Below, you will find reference to many of the icings, colourings and edible decorations you can buy, as well as, following on, key icing recipes which will show you how to whip up your own icings and moulding pastes from scratch. These ingredients and icings will be referenced often throughout the main recipe chapters.

~ Icing Sugar – Icing sugar is fine and powdery. It is usually sold plain and white, but can also be bought as an unrefined golden (or 'natural') variety. Use it for delicate icings, frostings and decorations. Store this sugar in a dry place, as it can absorb moisture and this will make it go hard and lumpy. Always sift this sugar at least once, or preferably twice, before you use it, to remove any hard lumps that would prevent icing from achieving a smooth texture – lumpy icing is impossible to pipe out.

~ Fondant Icing Sugar – This is sold in plain and flavoured varieties and gives a beautiful glossy finish to cake toppings. Just add a little boiled water to the sugar, according to the packet instructions, to make a shiny icing that can be poured or drizzled over cake tops to give a very professional finish. Colour the plain white icing with a few spots of paste food colouring to achieve your desired result.

Flavoured fondant icing sugar is sold in strawberry, raspberry, orange, lemon and blackcurrant flavours and also has colouring added. These are ideal if you want to make a large batch of cakes with different coloured and flavoured toppings. Fondant sugars can also be whisked with softened unsalted butter and cream cheese to make delicious frostings in just a few moments.

∾ Royal Icing Sugar – Royal icing sets to a classic, firm Christmas-cake-style covering or can be made to a softer consistency to give a glossy finish. Sold in packs as plain white sugar, this is whisked with cold water to give an instant royal icing. It has dried egg white included in the mixture, so does not need the long beating that traditional royal icing recipes require. It is also ideal to use for those who cannot eat raw egg whites.

∾ Gum Tragacanth – This is a powder used to strengthen sugarpaste to make a firmer texture. Buy it from specialist cake-decorating stores.

∾ Tubes of Writing Icing – You can buy small tubes of ready-coloured royal icing or gel icing, usually in sets of black, red, yellow and blue, and these are ideal for small amounts of writing or for piping on dots or small decorations.

∾ Cold Boiled Water – This is used for sticking pieces of sugarpaste together. Keep a small bottle handy for projects.

∾ Confectioner's Glaze – Sold in small tubs, this is used to give a shiny finish to models. Paint the glaze directly onto the model and leave time for the glaze to dry out before adding to the cake.

∾ Piping Gel – This is a transparent gel used to make small shiny dots to represent raindrops on flower models. It can be bought from specialist cake-decorating stores. To use, pipe on in small balls to add sparkle to flowers and leaves.

Decorating Ingredients

Edible Glue or Gum Glue – When you need something a little stronger than cold boiled water to stick pieces together, you can use edible glue. Buy commercial edible glue from specialist cake-decorating stores or make your own sugar glue.

Sugar Glue – Make your own sugar glue by breaking up small pieces of modelling paste and placing them in a small container. Cover with boiling water and stir until dissolved. If the glue is too thick, thin down using a little cold boiled water.

Rejuvenator Spirit or Vodka – These should be used with lustres and coloured dusts (see below). Either paint the surface to be covered or mix the lustre powder with the spirit to make a thin paint. Both spirit and vodka will dry out quickly and give a translucent sheen to colours and metallic finishes. Don't mix lustre powders with cold boiled water, as this takes longer to dry out and will give a sticky, muddy finish.

Food Colourings – You can buy food colourings in a great range of colours, in liquid, paste, gel and powder or dust forms:

Paste food colourings are best for using with sugarpaste. These are sold in small tubs and are very concentrated, so should be added to the sugarpaste dot by dot on the end of a wooden cocktail stick. Knead the colouring in evenly, adding more until you get the colour you require.

Dusts and lustre colourings are sold in small pots and come in a large range of colours, from very bright to delicate shades, and can also be bought in pearl, silver and gold shades. The fine dust should be lightly brushed onto surfaces that have been previously painted with rejuvenator spirit or vodka. Use a paintbrush to form a delicate sheen to decorations such as tips of petals and the centres of flowers. You can also make a liquid paint from lustre powder by mixing with a little rejuvenator spirit or vodka.

Metallic finishes can be achieved by using edible liquid metallic paint for small items. For larger areas, spray-on metallic colours are sold in small aerosol cans and these can be used to ensure an even, glossy sheen.

Food colouring pens are handy for details on models, such as for highlighting small areas like eyes and lips on faces, or for shading flowers and making patterns. Buy a set of coloured edible-ink pens from specialist cake-decorating stores.

Coloured sugars can be made by adding a few dots of paste colouring to granulated sugar with a toothpick. Coloured sugars add sparkle to the sides of cakes, cookies and cupcakes.

∾ Bought Sugar Decorations and Sprinkles – A range of sprinkles in all sorts of colours, shapes and finishes can be bought in supermarkets or by mail order from specialist cake-decorating companies, and these provide a wonderful way to make quick and easy cake toppings. They enhance texture as well as looks.

Decorating Ingredients

Apricot Glaze Almond Paste

Makes 450 g/1 lb to cover 2 x 20 cm/8 inch round cakes, or 24 small cakes

For the apricot glaze:

450 g/1 lb apricot jam
3 tbsp water
1 tsp lemon juice

For the almond paste:

125 g/4 oz sifted icing sugar
125 g/4 oz caster sugar
225 g/8 oz ground almonds
1 medium egg
1 tsp lemon juice

For the apricot glaze, place the jam, water and juice in a heavy-based saucepan and heat gently, stirring, until soft and melted.

Boil rapidly for 1 minute, then press through a fine sieve with the back of a wooden spoon. Discard the pieces of fruit.

Use immediately for glazing or sticking on almond paste, or pour into a clean jar or plastic airtight container and store in the refrigerator for up to 3 months.

For the almond paste, stir the sugars and ground almonds together in a bowl. Whisk the egg and lemon juice together and mix into the dry ingredients.

Knead until the paste is smooth. Wrap tightly in clingfilm or foil to keep airtight and store in the refrigerator until needed. The paste can be made 2–3 days ahead of time, but, after that, it will start to dry out and become difficult to handle.

To use the paste, knead on a surface dusted with icing sugar. Brush the top of each cake with apricot glaze. Roll out the almond paste to a circle large enough to cover the cake or cut out discs large enough to cover the tops of the cupcakes. Press onto the cakes. For how to cover large cakes with almond paste, see page 42.

Basic Buttercream Frosting

Covers a 20 cm/8 inch round cake or 12 small cakes

Ingredients

150 g/5 oz unsalted butter, softened at room temperature
225 g/8 oz icing sugar, sifted
2 tbsp hot milk or water
1 tsp vanilla extract
food colourings of choice

Beat the butter until light and fluffy, then beat in the sifted icing sugar and hot milk or water in two batches.

Add the vanilla extract and any colourings. Store chilled for up to 2 days in an airtight container.

Variations
Omit the vanilla extract and instead:

∽ Coffee – Blend 2 tsp coffee extract with the milk.

∽ Chocolate – Blend 2 tbsp cocoa powder to a paste with 2 tbsp boiling water and use instead of the hot milk or water.

∽ Lemon – Beat in 1 tbsp fresh lemon juice, sieved.

Cream Cheese Frosting

Covers a 20 cm/8 inch
round cake
or 12 small cakes

Ingredients

50 g/2 oz unsalted butter,
softened at room temperature
300 g/11 oz icing sugar, sifted
flavouring of choice
food colourings of choice
125 g/4 oz full-fat cream cheese

Beat the butter and icing sugar together until light and fluffy.

Add flavourings and colourings of choice and beat again.

Add the cream cheese and whisk until light and fluffy.

Do not overbeat, however, as the mixture can become runny.

Sugarpaste Icing
(a.k.a. Fondant for Rolling or Modelling)

Makes 350 g/12 oz to cover a
20 cm/8 inch round cake
or 12 small cakes, or use
for decorations

Ingredients

1 medium egg white
1 tbsp liquid glucose
350 g/12 oz icing sugar, sifted,
plus extra for dusting

Place the egg white and liquid glucose in a large mixing bowl and stir together, breaking up the egg white.

Add the icing sugar gradually, mixing in until the mixture binds together and forms a ball.

Turn the ball of icing out onto a clean surface dusted with icing sugar and knead for 5 minutes until soft but firm enough to roll out. If the icing is too soft, knead in a little more icing sugar until the mixture is pliable.

To colour, knead in paste food colouring. Do not use liquid food colouring, as this is not suitable and will make the sugarpaste limp.

To use, roll out thinly on a clean surface dusted with icing sugar to a circle large enough to cover a cake or cut out discs large enough to cover the top of each cupcake.

∽ Strengthened Sugarpaste – Some larger models will require using strengthened sugarpaste. This is a combination of half sugarpaste and half flower paste (*see* page 22) kneaded together to make a smooth paste that will harden more firmly than normal sugarpaste, yet will be soft enough to cut through. Keep tightly wrapped in clingfilm, then wrap in a plastic bag to exclude any air. Use strengthened paste to make plaques or large areas that require a firmer paste.

Flower Paste

Ingredients

2 tsp powdered gelatine
2 tsp liquid glucose
2 tsp white vegetable fat
450 g/1 lb sifted icing sugar
1 tsp gum tragacanth
1 egg white

Flower, petal or 'gum' paste is used for making very thin, delicate flowers and decorations, which set hard so that they can be handled easily.

Flower paste will roll out much more thinly than sugarpaste and is worth using for wedding cakes, as it gives a realistic finish to flowers, and these can be made ahead of time and easily stored. It can be bought from cake-decorating suppliers or by mail order in small, ready-made slabs in different colours or as a powder that can be reconstituted with a little cold water and made into a paste.

To make your own, follow the recipe and store the paste in the refrigerator, tightly wrapped in strong plastic until needed.

Place 1½ tsp cold water in a heatproof bowl. Sprinkle over the gelatine and add the liquid glucose and white fat. Place the bowl over a saucepan of hot water and heat until melted, stirring occasionally. Cool slightly.

Sift the icing sugar and gum tragacanth into a bowl, make a well in the centre and add the egg white and the cooled gelatine mixture. Mix together to make a soft paste.

Knead the paste on a surface dusted with icing sugar until smooth, then wrap in clingfilm to exclude all air. Leave for 2 hours, then break off small pieces and use to make fine flowers and petals.

Modelling Paste

Ingredients

225 g/8 oz ready-to-roll sugarpaste
5 ml/1 tsp gum tragacanth

This is ideal for moulding, as it has a firm but elastic texture. A versatile paste, it keeps its shape well and dries harder than sugarpaste. Buy it commercially from cake-decorating stores or make your own version, as here.

Roll the sugarpaste until soft, then make a dip in the middle. Add the gum tragacanth to the dip and knead in until smooth and thoroughly combined.

Wrap the sugarpaste tightly in clingfilm, then in a plastic bag and leave to stand overnight to achieve a pliable texture. Keep the paste wrapped and break off small pieces, kneading well to make it flexible before use.

Royal Icing

Makes 500 g/1 lb 2 oz to cover a 20 cm/8 inch round cake or 12 small cakes

Ingredients

2 medium egg whites
500 g/1 lb 2 oz icing sugar, sifted
2 tsp lemon juice

Put the egg whites in a large bowl and whisk lightly with a fork to break up the whites until foamy.

Sift in half the icing sugar with the lemon juice and beat well with an electric mixer for 4 minutes, or by hand with a wooden spoon for about 10 minutes, until smooth.

Gradually sift in the remaining icing sugar and beat again until thick, smooth and brilliant white and the icing forms soft peaks when flicked up with a spoon.

Keep the royal icing covered with a clean, damp cloth until ready for use, or store in the refrigerator in an airtight plastic container until needed.

If making royal icing to use later, beat it again before use to remove any air bubbles that may have formed in the mixture.

Modelling Chocolate

Ingredients

125 g/4 oz plain, milk or
white chocolate
2 tbsp liquid glucose

Break the chocolate into small pieces and melt in a heatproof bowl standing over a pan of very gently simmering water.

Remove from the heat and beat in the liquid glucose until a paste forms that comes away from the sides of the bowl.

Place the paste in a plastic bag and chill for 1 hour until firm, or store for up to 2 weeks in a tightly sealed plastic bag.

To use, break off pieces and knead until pliable. Modelling chocolate is ideal for making thin ribbons and flowers.

Chocolate Covering Icing

To cover a 20 cm/8 inch round cake

Ingredients

175 g/6 oz dark chocolate
2 tbsp liquid glucose
1 medium egg white
500 g/1 lb 2 oz sifted icing sugar

Break up the chocolate into pieces and melt in a heatproof bowl standing over a bowl of very gently simmering water. Add the liquid glucose and stir until melted.

Remove from the heat and cool for 5 minutes, then whisk in the egg white and half the sugar until smooth. When the mixture becomes stiff, turn out onto a flat surface and knead in the remaining icing sugar.

Wrap tightly in clingfilm and keep in a cool place for up to 3 days. To use, break off pieces and knead until soft and warm. Use quickly, as, when the paste cools, it will start to harden more quickly than sugarpaste.

Glacé Icing

Covers a 20 cm/8 inch
round cake (top)
or 12 small cakes

Ingredients

225 g/8 oz icing sugar
few drops lemon juice, vanilla or
almond extract
2–3 tbsp boiling water
liquid or paste
food colouring (optional)

Sift the icing sugar into a bowl and add the chosen flavouring, then gradually stir in enough water to mix to the consistency of thick cream.

Beat with a wooden spoon until the icing is thick enough to coat the back of the spoon, and add a few drops of liquid or paste food colouring, if desired. Use immediately, as the icing will begin to form a skin as it starts to set.

Sugarcraft Equipment

c

If you are to produce the best results possible, sugarcraft and cake decorating require a fair few more pieces of equipment than standard baking!

- **Cake Boards** – Thin and thicker drum-style boards are needed to give the cakes a good base.

- **Dowels** – Cake dowels (*see* left) are small, short pieces of thin plastic or wood that are used to support tiers of cake. Four dowels are usually inserted into a cake base at equal distances to support the next layer placed on top.

- **Turntable** – A heavy-based icing turntable (*see* left) helps you coat the sides of a cake easily. A tilting turntable – a turntable with a cranked base that will allow you to tilt the cake to eye level – is useful for adding difficult designs to the sides of cakes.

- **Plastic Rolling Pins** – A long plastic rolling pin is needed for easy rolling out of sugarpaste. Wooden pins can be used for almond paste but are not good for sugarpaste, which tends to stick to them. A small plastic rolling pin is useful for rolling out small quantities of flower paste.

- **Textured Rolling Pins** – These plastic pins will imprint patterns into sugarpaste as they roll. They come with spacers, which can be added to each end of the pin to give different widths of pattern.

- Boards – Large plastic boards are useful if you do not have a nonstick kitchen surface, and small plastic boards are vital for rolling out small pieces of flower paste.

- Paint Brushes – A selection of fine-tipped paintbrushes (*see* right) should be kept just for adding painted-on details to sugarpaste projects.

- Stippling Brushes – These wide, flat brushes are used for flicking lustre dust over models or for brushing powders directly onto surfaces to make a stippled or marbled effect.

- Small Foam Pad – Use this for pressing petals out into curved and frilled shapes and for moulding blossom and small flowers.

- Clingfilm and Plastic Food Bags – These are needed to wrap sugarpaste, modelling or flower paste tightly to prevent it from drying out. If you need to colour lots of small pieces of paste, wrap them tightly in clingfilm, then pack into food bags to keep airtight.

- Icing Sleeve or Wallet – A large, flat, plastic double-sided sleeve is used for making large numbers of petals or flowers. Slices of sugarpaste, marzipan or chocolate modelling paste can be pressed out from the sleeve, keeping the remainder covered to keep them soft and pliable. A firm, clear document wallet makes a good sleeve.

- Wooden Cocktail Sticks – Cocktail sticks or toothpicks (*see* right) are used for colouring, rolling and fluting scraps of flower paste and lifting delicate pieces of sugarpaste into position. They are also useful for securing items such as heads and heavy limbs on sugar models. Always remove before serving or tell your guests to do so before eating – especially when children are concerned.

Sugarcraft Equipment

Scissors – A separate small pair of sharp, pointed scissors is needed for snipping into sugarpaste and shaping with the pointed ends.

Smoothers – Smoothers (*see* left) are essential for achieving a smooth finish on a sugarpaste-covered cake. Holding one in each hand will give a perfect top and sides to a cake.

Spirit Level – A spirit level is needed for tiered cakes such as wedding cakes, to check that the tiers are even and level.

Garlic or Icing Press – A press (*see* left) is used to achieve long strands of sugarpaste, such as hair on models.

Wooden Spoon Handles and Spaghetti – Use wooden spoon handles wrapped in clingfilm for shaping ribbons and bows. Use short pieces of spaghetti for shaping difficult small areas.

Tweezers – A pair of tweezers is useful for positioning small, delicate items in place or for making a rough pattern in sugarpaste.

Pins – Glass-headed dressmakers' pins keep templates in place.

Wires – 20- and 26-gauge sugarcraft wires can be used for securing the stems and stalks of flowers

Floristry Tape & Foam – This paper tape (*see* left; also known as 'stem tape') is used to cover bunches of wires to avoid contact between the wires and the cake. It also creates a more realistic finish and holds together multiple stems to create sprays of flowers. You usually have to cut the tape to half its width. Attach the tape to the top of the stem and then wind down, twizzling the stem in your hand as you go. A block of floristry foam is useful for keeping flowers on wires upright while they dry.

~ Stamens – Small bunches of stamens on fine wires (*see* right) form the centres of dainty flowers such as blossom. These are inserted into the centres of each sugar flower and then the flowers can be wired and wrapped in floristry tape.

~ Silicone Moulds – These are soft, flexible moulds made in the shape of flowers, leaves, lace etc, that can be filled with flower paste, which is then pushed out to give an instant shaped decoration (*see* centre right).

~ Veining Mat – A veining mat or mould is usually made from flexible silicone and is used for adding lifelike details to leaves and petals. They come in a variety of patterns, but a basic leaf veiner will be useful. Some veiners come as double-sided moulds and these give a really lifelike appearance to leaves.

~ Resin Embossing Moulds – These are firm moulds that are pressed into sugarpaste to make detailed decorations such as lace borders. To make the paste easier to remove from the mould, lightly dust the mould first with cornflour or icing sugar.

~ Resin Bead Moulds – These firm moulds (*see* bottom right) are used to create evenly shaped strings of beads and pearls. They have two sides and the paste is pressed into the mould to create perfect round beads, ovals or other decorative beading.

~ Stamps and Cutters – Cutters for cutting out intricate icing shapes can be bought from specialist cake and baking stores. Like normal cookie cutters, they come in classic metal styles, in plastic, or as plunger-style. If you do not have appropriate cutters, there are some templates at the back of this book that can be used instead.

Sugarcraft Equipment

Flower cutters are necessary to cut out petals, blossom and leaves from flower paste. You will need a selection of flower cutters made from plastic or metal. A good basic selection will include small, medium and large blossom cutters, a selection of daisy, star flowers and Tudor rose cutters and some basic petal and leaf cutters.

Tappit cutters are used to cut out fine shapes like letters and numbers or small detailed decorations that need to be repeated.

Ribbon cutters/rollers are used to make cutting strips of rolled-out sugarpaste into ribbons as accurate as possible. A multi-ribbon cutter will have a handle with interchangeable cutters that will cut wide or narrow widths or decorative edging.

Cutting wheels are very useful for cutting rolled-out sugarpaste freehand into strips and shapes. They can be used for making fine fringes or, lightly pressed onto models, they can make freehand designs. They come with plain or patterned edges for different designs.

∾ Small Plastic Bottles – Small reusable plastic storage bottles with pointed tips are handy for keeping different colours of royal icing for piping onto surfaces.

∾ Ribbons – Satin or floristry paper ribbons give each cake a flourish and can finish over any mistakes or defects.

∾ Print Wrap – Patterns can be printed on edible paper or rice paper. Edible printed ribbons can be bought from cake-decorating specialists.

Sugarpaste Tools

∽ **Balling Tool** (1) – A balling tool is invaluable for making rounded shapes and impressions.

∽ **Cone Tool** (2) – These tapered tools come with smooth and serrated ends. Uses include hollowing out tubular flowers and adding texture.

∽ **Bone Tool** (3) – A bone tool has a large and a smaller rounded, curved end that protrude outwards and these will help you to model hollow shapes in balls of sugarpaste or curved cup shapes in petals and flowers.

∽ **Comb and Scallop Tool** (4) – A comb tool (top end of the tool in the picture) can be used to score parallel lines or mark a serrated design, such as stitching. A scallop tool (bottom end) is handy for marking on features such as smiling or frowning mouths, eyebrows and ears, and also is useful as a mini scoop for distributing sprinkles accurately.

∽ **Blade Tool** (5) – Use this tool to cut, shape and mark on lines.

∽ **Fluting Tool** (6) – This creates open centres in cut-out shapes.

∽ **Star Tool** (7) – This creates ridged shapes in the centres of flowers and also doubles as an embossing tool.

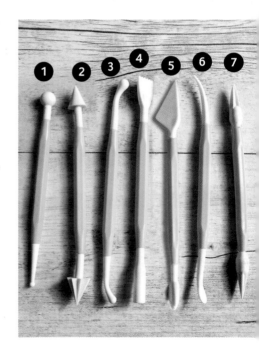

Sugarcraft Equipment

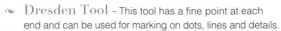
Dresden Tool – This tool has a fine point at each end and can be used for marking on dots, lines and details.

Shell Tool (8) – A shell tool embosses shell patterns and shapes shell borders.

Scriber (9) – A scriber needle or pin tool is used for marking out lettering or patterns on your cake.

Quilting Tool – A quilting tool is needed for straight lines and stitching effects.

Cutting Wheel – This is used for cutting sugarpaste and flower paste in a wide variety of patterns. You can use a crimped-edge pasta cutting wheel for a crimped effect.

Crimping Tools (10) – Operated like tweezers, crimpers with different edges give finishes like heart shapes, swags and quilted-line effects, making it easy to create a neat, consistent border around a cake.

Flower Nail – A flower nail, which looks like an oversized nail with a flat, wide head, is used for making piped royal iced or buttercream flowers. A square of waxed paper is attached to the 'head' of the 'nail' and the nail is turned as the petals are piped out onto the paper. It can also be used to help a large cake cook more evenly – by placing it upside down in the centre of the tin before pouring in the batter, it will conduct heat to the centre of the cake. Be sure to grease or line the tin over the top of the nail.

Piping Bags and Nozzles

- **Fabric Bags** – A nylon piping bag that comes with a set of five nozzles is a very useful piece of equipment for decorating with icings. Look for a set with a plain nozzle and various star nozzles for piping swirls. The larger the star nozzle, the wider the swirls will be on the finished cake. Nylon piping bags can be washed out in warm soapy water and dried out, ready to reuse again and again.

- **Disposable Bags** – Paper or clear plastic icing bags are available and are quick and easy to use. Clear plastic piping bags are useful for piping large swirls on cupcakes.

- **Make a Paper Icing Bag** – Cut out a 38 x 25.5 cm/15 x 10 inch rectangle of greaseproof paper. Fold it diagonally in half to form two triangular shapes. Cut along the fold line to make two triangles. One of these triangles can be used another time – it is quicker and easier to make two at a time from one square than to measure and mark out a triangle on a sheet of paper.

Fold one of the points of the long side of the triangle over itself to make a sharp cone and hold in the centre (*see* centre right). Fold the other sharp end of the triangle over the cone. Hold all the layers together at the back of the cone, keeping the pointed end sharp. Fold the points into the cone (*see* bottom right), smoothing to make a crease, then secure with a piece of sticky tape.

To use, snip away the end, place a piping nozzle in position and fill the bag with icing, or fill the bag first, then snip away a tiny hole at the end for piping a plain edge, writing or piping tiny dots.

Sugarcraft Equipment

Sugarcraft Techniques

Covering a Cake with Almond Paste

Almond paste (*see* page 14) gives a base layer over which to cover a cake with icing, giving a smooth, flat surface that encloses the cake and keeps it moist. Rich fruit cakes need to be covered in almond paste to cover the dark cake and improve its keeping qualities.

First, remove all the papers in which the cake was baked, and trim the top of the cake level if it has peaked. Brush the top and sides of the cake with apricot glaze (*see* page 14).

Sprinkle a clean flat surface with icing sugar and knead one third of the almond paste. Roll out to the same shape as the top of the cake and lay the paste on top.

Measure the circumference of the cake or the length of one side with a piece of string. Knead the remaining paste and, using the string as a guide, roll the paste into a strip long enough to go round the cake and wide enough to cover the sides. Roll the paste up into a coil and press one end onto the side of the cake. Unroll the paste, pressing into the sides of the cake as you go round. Press the top and sides together to join them.

Flatten the top and sides with a small rolling pin or an icing smoother and leave to dry out for 24 hours before icing and decorating.

Using Buttercream and Cream Cheese Frostings

These soft icings can be swirled onto the tops of cakes with a small palette knife or placed in a piping bag fitted with a star nozzle to pipe impressive whirls, such as when you want to finish off your cake with a piped border or simply add those elegant flourishes.

Keep cakes with frostings in a cool place, or refrigerate, as they contain a high percentage of butter, which will melt easily in too warm a place.

∾ **Covering a Cake with Frosting** – Do not be mean with the amount of frosting you use. If this is scraped on thinly, you will see the cake underneath, so be generous.

If your cake has a dark crumb base, such as a chocolate cake, place it in the freezer for 15 minutes before spreading over the buttercream, to give a firm base that will keep the crumbs from spreading into the buttercream.

Place a generous amount in the centre of the cake and spread this over the top with a large, flat-bladed knife or a palette knife. Spread over the sides separately and tidy up the edges with an icing scraper.

∾ **Piping Buttercream onto Cupcakes** – Take a large piping bag and add the nozzle of your choice. A star nozzle will give a whirly effect and a plain nozzle will create a smooth, coiled effect. Half-fill the bag, shake down the buttercream and fill the bag again. Twist the top round to seal tightly. Squeeze the bag until the buttercream comes out. Start on the outer edge and gently squeeze the buttercream out in one continuous spiral. Lift the bag away to give a peaked finish to the top.

∾ **Decorating Buttercream** – Cakes coated in buttercream can be decorated easily with colourful sprinkles and sugars. This is easy

Sugarcraft Techniques

with cupcakes. Place the sprinkles in a small saucer or on a piece of nonstick baking parchment and roll the outside edges of each cupcake in the decorations.

Using Sugarpaste

Sugarpaste is a versatile icing, as it can be used for covering whole cakes or modelling all sorts of fancy decorations.

- ❧ Paste food colourings are best for working with sugarpaste and a little goes a very long way. As these are very concentrated, use a cocktail stick to add dots of paste gradually, until you are sure of the colour, and knead in until even.

- ❧ Always roll out almond paste or sugarpaste on a surface lightly dusted with icing sugar. Use cornflour for rolling out flower paste, as this needs to be kept dry and flexible and adding extra sugar to the liquid glucose and gelatine in flower paste can make it sticky.

- ❧ Leave sugarpaste-covered cakes to firm up for 2 hours before adding decorations, as this provides a good finished surface to work on.

- ❧ Once decorated, store sugarpaste-covered cakes in large boxes in a cool place. Do not store in a refrigerator, as the sugarpaste will become damp and colours may run.

- ❧ Covering a Large Cake with Sugarpaste Icing – Spread buttercream or apricot glaze over the trimmed cake to give a surface for the sugarpaste to stick to, or, If covered in almond paste, brush the paste lightly with a little boiled water.

Knead the sugarpaste until softened, then roll into a ball. Roll out to about 1 cm/$^{1}/_{2}$ inch thickness on a flat surface lightly dusted with icing sugar, moving the sugarpaste occasionally to prevent it from sticking to the surface.

Take a piece of string and measure the distance across the top and down either side of the cake and cut the sugarpaste 2.5 cm/1 inch larger in order to cover the whole cake. Lift the sugarpaste carefully onto the cake, holding it flat with your palms until it is central.

Dust your hands with icing sugar and smooth the icing down over the top and sides of the cake, fluting out the bottom edges. Do not pleat the icing, as this will leave lines. Smooth down to remove any air bubbles under the surface of the icing, then trim the edges with a sharp knife.

Using the flat of your hand or an icing smoother, flatten out the top and sides using a circular movement. Do not wear any rings, as these will leave ridges in the soft icing. Gather up the trimmings into a ball and keep these tightly wrapped in a plastic bag.

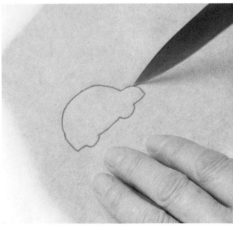

∾ To Cover Cupcakes – Cut out circles the size of the cupcake tops. Coat each cake with a little apricot glaze or buttercream and press on the circles to form a flat surface.

∾ To Copy Patterns from Templates onto Sugarpaste – At the back of this book, you will find templates for some of the shapes used in the recipes. Trace the pattern you want onto a sheet of clear greaseproof paper or nonstick baking parchment.

∾   Sugarcraft Techniques

Roll out the sugarpaste thinly, then position the traced pattern on top. Mark over the pattern with the tip of a small, sharp knife or a pin. Remove the paper and cut out the marked-on pattern with a small, sharp knife.

∞ Making Flat Decorations – To make letters, numbers or flat decorations, roll out the sugarpaste thinly and cut out the shapes. Leave to dry on nonstick baking parchment on a flat surface or a tray for 2–3 hours to make them firm and easy to handle.

∞ Making Bows – Roll out the sugarpaste thinly on a surface lightly dusted with icing sugar and, with a knife, cut out long, thin, narrow strips.

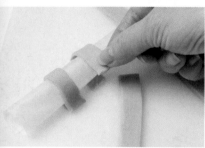

Roll small squares of baking parchment into narrow tubes, or line the handle of a wooden spoon with clingfilm. Fold the icing over the paper or handle to form loops and leave to dry and harden for 2 hours, then carefully remove the paper or spoon handle.

To make bows that are placed directly onto the cake, fill the centre of each loop with cotton wool balls, then remove these when the icing is firm.

∞ Making Roses – Colour the sugarpaste icing with pink paste food colouring. Take a small piece of sugarpaste and make a small cone shape, then roll a small pea-size piece of sugarpaste into a ball. Flatten out the ball into a petal shape and wrap this round the cone shape.

Continue adding more petals, then trim the thick base. Leave to dry for 2 hours in a clean egg box lined with foil or clingfilm.

Making Lilies – Lilies of all sizes and colours can make elegant decorations for cakes (*see* Calla Lilies, page 100, for example).

Colour a little sugarpaste a deep yellow and mould this into thin sausage shapes. Leave these to firm on nonstick baking parchment or clingfilm for 2 hours.

Thinly roll out white sugarpaste and mark out small squares of 4 x 4 cm/1½ x 1½ inches. Wrap each square round a yellow centre to form a lily and press the ends together. Place the lilies on nonstick baking parchment to dry out for 2 hours.

Making Daisies – Daisies of all sizes are a popular flower to be found on decorated cakes.

To model from sugarpaste, roll out a little sugarpaste thinly and, using a daisy stamp cutter, press out small flower shapes and mould these into a curve.

Leave the daisies to dry out on nonstick baking parchment, then pipe dots into the centre of each one with yellow royal icing or a small gel tube of writing icing.

Making Butterfly Wings – Colour the sugarpaste and roll out thinly. Trace round the butterfly patterns and cut out the wing shapes. Leave these to dry flat on nonstick baking parchment for 4 hours to make them firm and easy to lift.

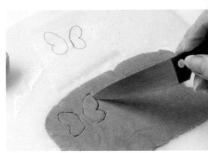

Making Ruffles – To make frills and ruffles, roll out the sugarpaste on a surface lightly dusted with icing sugar and

Sugarcraft Techniques

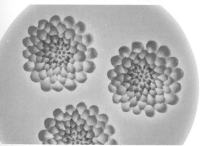

stamp out a fluted circle 6 cm/2¹/₂ inches wide with a pastry cutter. Cut away a small, plain disc 2.5 cm/1 inch wide from the centre, and discard. Take a cocktail stick and roll this back and forth until the sugarpaste begins to frill up.

∽ Using Silicone Moulds – Push-up silicone moulds have made cake decorating so easy, as all you have to do is press a little sugarpaste into the mould and then press this out and you will have a beautiful ready-made decoration. You can buy these moulds online from sugarcraft specialists or from hobby and craft shops. You will find a huge selection in all sorts of shapes and sizes – flowers, borders, buttons, toys and novelties of all types.

To make a moulded shape, roll out an appropriately-sized ball of sugarpaste on a surface dusted with icing sugar until pliable. Make sure the mould is clean and dry and dust it with a little icing sugar. Gently push the paste into the mould. Don't force it too hard or it will clog the mould.

Turn the mould over and flex it until the sugarpaste shape drops out. Repeat until you have the number of shapes needed, then leave these to dry out overnight on a sheet of nonstick baking parchment.

∽ Using Embossing Tools and Mats to Decorate – Embossing tools make lacy impressions and designs on sugarpaste. These come as stamps or plastic strips with a raised impression and are pushed into the soft paste to make the pattern. They can be used in conjunction with lustre powders to make a two-tone effect.

Using Royal Icing

- **Covering a Cake with Royal Icing** – Make sure the almond paste has dried out for 24 hours, or oil from the paste may seep into the icing. Place a large spoonful of icing in the centre of the cake and smooth out using a palette knife in a paddling movement to get rid of any air bubbles.

  Draw an icing rule across the top of the cake towards you at an angle. Repeat, pulling back and forth, until the icing is flat. Remove any surplus icing round the top edges and leave to dry out for 24 hours. Keep the remaining icing covered in an airtight plastic box. To cover the sides, for best results, place the cake on an icing turntable. Spread a layer of icing round the sides, using the same paddling motion as for the top. Smooth the surface roughly, then, holding an icing scraper at a 45-degree angle, rotate the cake, keeping the scraper still. Rotate the cake until the sides are flat, then carefully lift away any excess icing with a palette knife to give a clean top edge. Leave to dry out for 24 hours. Repeat, adding another layer of icing to give a smooth surface for decorating.

- **Piping Royal Icing Borders** – Fit a small paper icing bag with a star or a straight nozzle and fill the bag three-quarters full with royal icing. Fold over the top and push out a little of the icing at right angles to the base of the cake. As the icing is pushed out, reduce the pressure and lift the bag away. Continue piping another shape next to the first one, until you have completed the border round the base of the cake. You can use the same technique for piping buttercream onto cakes, but this will be a little softer to pipe out and requires less pressure.

- **Piping Flowers on a Flower Nail** – Cut small squares of waxed paper and attach each to a flower nail with a dot of royal icing.

  To pipe a rose, half-fill a small piping bag fitted with a petal nozzle and, holding the nozzle at a right angle to the paper, with the thinnest part uppermost, pipe a small cone onto the paper to form the rosebud. Pipe petals round the rosebud onto the paper, overlapping

Sugarcraft Techniques

each one and curling the edge away. Leave the roses to dry out for 12 hours, then peel away from the paper to use, or store in an airtight container between layers of baking parchment until needed.

To pipe a daisy, work with the thick edge of the nozzle towards the centre and pipe five even-sized petals so that they meet in a star shape. Pipe a round dot in the centre in a contrasting colour and leave to dry out as above.

Using Glacé Icing

A quick and easy way to cover cakes and cookies is by using glacé icing. This is just a paste made from icing sugar and water until a coating consistency is formed. Liquid or paste food colourings can be added to glacé and it needs to be used immediately, as it will start to set once spread. Add any sprinkles or decorations to the wet glacé icing immediately, or sprinkle over chopped nuts or cherries.

To make a feathered effect in glacé icing, colour one batch of icing, then colour a little icing in a contrasting colour and place this in a small paper icing bag. Spread the main colour over the cake or cookie and then pipe a pattern onto the wet icing and pull a wooden toothpick through this immediately to give a feathered effect. Work quickly while the icing is wet and then leave to dry and set for 1 hour.

Using Chocolate

~ Melting Chocolate – Care and attention is needed to melt chocolate for baking and cake-decorating needs. If the chocolate gets too hot or comes into contact with water or steam, it will 'seize' or stiffen and form into a hard ball instead of a smooth melted mixture. You can add a little vegetable oil or margarine, a teaspoon at a time, to the mixture to make it liquid again.

To melt chocolate, break the bar into small pieces, or grate or chop it, and place in a heatproof bowl standing over a bowl of warm, not hot, water. Make sure the bowl containing the chocolate is completely dry and that steam or water cannot enter the bowl. Heat the water to a gentle simmer only, and leave the bowl to stand for about 5 minutes. Do not let the water get too hot or the chocolate will reach too high a temperature and will lose its sheen.

The microwave oven is ideal for melting chocolate. Place the chocolate pieces in a small microwave-proof bowl and melt gently on low or defrost settings in small bursts of 30 seconds, checking and stirring in between, until the chocolate has melted.

∞ Covering Cupcakes with Melted Chocolate – If the cakes have domes, trim them neatly. While the chocolate is still warm, pour a little over each cupcake. Take each cake and gently tap on a surface to spread the icing to the edges of the cases. Add sprinkles or decorations and leave to set for 1 hour.

∞ Covering a Cake with Chocolate – Trim the cake level if necessary, then place on a wire rack over a tray. Pour the warm melted chocolate over and, working quickly, spread the chocolate over the top and sides with a palette knife. Patch up any bare areas and leave to set for 1 hour. Add any decorations while the icing is still wet and leave to dry.

🍂   Sugarcraft Techniques

∞ Curls – To make curls, melt the chocolate following your preferred method and then spread it in a thin layer over a cool surface, such as a marble slab, ceramic tile or piece of granite. Leave until just set but not hard. Take a clean paint scraper or knife and set it at an angle to the surface of the chocolate, then push, taking a layer off the surface. This will curl until you release the pressure.

∞ Caraque – Caraque are long, thin curls. To make caraque, prepare the chocolate in the same way as for the curls. Use a large, sharp knife and hold it at about a 45-degree angle to the chocolate. Hold the handle and the tip and scrape the knife towards you, pulling the handle but keeping the tip more or less in the same place. This method makes thinner, tighter, longer curls.

∞ Shaved Chocolate – Using a vegetable peeler, shave a thick block of chocolate to make mini curls. These are best achieved if the chocolate is a little soft, otherwise it has a tendency to break into little flakes.

∞ Chocolate Shapes – Spread a thin layer of chocolate, as described in the instructions for chocolate curls, and allow to set as before. Use shaped cutters or a sharp knife to cut out shapes. Use to decorate your cakes.

Finishing Touches

You will find a huge selection of cake accessories in craft and hobby shops or online. These include edible jewels made from sugar, which add sparkle to large and small cakes. Edible pearls and diamonds can set off a wedding cake or more fun edible jewels can be a favourite for children's party cakes.

- **Glitter** comes in bright colours in pots and is sold as dust or granules with a shine. Dusting powders give a more subtle natural sheen to flowers and ribbons.

- **Printed Papers and Ribbons** made from edible rice paper can create a pretty effect and can be cut through when serving the cake.

- **Cupcake Paper Liners** made from cut-out paper lace can be wrapped around deep cupcakes for a special occasion.

- **Ribbons and Paper Lace Trims** can be found in abundance in craft and hobby shops or online cake-decorating suppliers. A colourful contrasting or complementary ribbon will set off a cake beautifully. Tie ribbons round the finished cake and secure them with a dab of royal icing. Never use pins on a cake.

- **Crystallising Petals, Leaves and Berries** – Wash and dry herbs and leaves such as rosemary sprigs and small bay leaves or berries such as cranberries. Separate edible petals from small flowers such as rosebuds and clean small flowers such as violets with a clean brush, but do not wash them. Beat 1 medium egg white with 2 tsp cold water until frothy. Paint a thin layer of egg white carefully over the items, then sprinkle lightly with caster sugar (*see* right), shaking to remove any excess. Leave to dry on a wire rack lined with nonstick baking parchment.

Sugarcraft Techniques

Stacking Tiered Cakes

For large tiered cakes, you will need to insert small sticks of wooden or plastic dowelling into the lower tiers to take the weight of the next layer and stop it sinking.

First decide where you need to position the dowels: cover the cake with almond paste and sugarpaste and place centrally on a board. Place a sheet of baking parchment over the cake, cut to the size of the top of the cake. Based on the size of the cake that is to stand on top, decide where you want the dowels to go and mark four equal dots in a square, centrally on the paper.

Replace the paper and mark through each dot with a skewer. Remove the paper and push a dowel down into the cake at each mark. Make a mark with a pencil on the dowel at the point where the dowel comes out of the cake. Pull the dowels out of the cake and, using a serrated knife, trim them to 1 mm/1/32 inch above the pencil mark. Replace the dowels in the cake and ensure these are all 1 mm above the surface of the cake. If not, trim them again, then place the next tier of the cake on top (this should be sitting on a thin cake board that fits its size). Repeat for any more tiers.

If you are going to transport a tiered cake, remember to take each tier in a separate cardboard cake box and assemble it at the venue. Do not ever think of trying to transport a tiered cake once it is stacked up – it will be too heavy and you may damage all your hard work.

Flowers

If you've ever wanted to impress somebody with your cake-decorating skills, making sugarcraft flowers is the best way to do it. Try your hand at making Tea Cup Roses or Spring Daffodils, or, if you really want to impress, try the delicate Open Rose. All the projects in this book focus on how to make the more complex sugarcraft items shown and do not cover the cake itself or the more basic cake covering and decoration, unless integral to the design.

Yellow Daylilies

Makes 3 daylilies

medium gauge white floristry wire
cut into 18 lengths 15 cm/6 inches
250 g/9 oz pale lemon yellow
flower paste (*see* page 22)
floristry tape
cornflour, for dusting
edible glue
rejuvenator spirit or vodka
bronze lustre or blossom tint
dusting powder
75 g/3 oz light leaf-green
ready-to-roll sugarpaste
(*see* page 20)
icing sugar, for dusting

Make the wired stamens: bend the end of a piece of wire to make a tiny loop. Smooth a small ball of flower paste over the loop to cover it, then press the paste between your fingertips to flatten. Place the wire in a block of floristry foam to harden for 3 hours. Repeat with the remaining wires. Join six wires together with the flower paste ends at the top and wrap floristry tape round from the base to halfway up. Repeat with the remaining 12 wires.

Roll the remaining flower paste thinly on a surface dusted with cornflour and cut out 18 petals using a lily petal cutter or mark round the template on page 251 and cut out with a knife. Mark a ridge down the centre of each petal with a blunt marking tool. Bend each petal round to curve it, then leave to harden for 6 hours on a shaping rack or crumpled foil.

Fan out the wired stamens and, using edible glue, attach six petals at the join where the tape meets the bare wires. Repeat with the remaining stamens and petals and leave to dry upside down for 2 hours until firm.

Paint the paste-covered stamen tips lightly with spirit or vodka, then dab the dusting powder onto the end of each. Mix a little powder with the spirit or vodka and paint tiny bronze dots onto the lily petals with the brush tip.

Roll out the green sugarpaste on a surface dusted with icing sugar and cut into long leaves. Arrange these on the cake, then place the lilies on top.

Ruffle Roses

Makes 12 roses

1/2 batch buttercream (*see* page 16)
pink paste food colouring

Colour the buttercream pink with a little paste food colouring. Place the buttercream in a small piping bag fitted with a flower petal piping nozzle. Place a small square of waxed paper on a flower nail and secure with a dab of buttercream. Pipe on a cone in the centre of the paper. Position the tube at right angles, with the wider end of the tube at the bottom and the thinner end at the top. Start squeezing the bag, turning the nail as you go to pipe out a coiled centre around the cone.

Start at the base and, applying pressure to the bag, lift the tube up and drop it back to the base to create the first petal. Pipe a second petal halfway along the first one, then another, turning the nail as you go.

Continue piping petals, making these more open by tilting the nail, not the piping nozzle. Create more petals, increasing the number of petals in each row until you have 10–12 petals.

Carefully slip the waxed paper square from the nail and leave the piped rose to dry for 30 minutes. Slide the rose from the waxed paper onto a cranked palette knife and position on the cake, securing with a dab of buttercream.

Note: You can use this technique to make royal iced roses. Use 1/2 batch pink royal icing and leave the roses to dry on the waxed papers for 24 hours until firm. Peel the papers away to use the roses for decoration.

Golden Mini Ribbon Rosebuds

Makes 12

175 g/6 oz ready-to-roll sugarpaste
(*see* page 20)
edible liquid gold food colouring

Shape the sugarpaste into a thin sausage shape, then flatten this out between your fingertips into a ribbon strip. Trim the strip to about 5 cm/2 inches long and 2 cm/^{3}/$_4$ inch wide and coil this up into a loose spiral shape. Cut the base flat and place the rosebud on nonstick baking parchment. Make 11 more rosebuds and leave them on the parchment for 30 minutes to firm up.

Using a small, fine paintbrush, paint the gold food colouring around the top of the rosebud. Paint all the rosebuds and leave to dry for 2 hours on nonstick baking parchment until the gold colouring is completely dry.

Using tweezers, lift each rosebud up carefully and place in the centre of a cream cheese-frosted cupcake just before serving.

Tip: Use silver metallic food colouring as an alternative or paint the roses with coloured tinted lustre powders mixed with rejuvenator spirit or vodka.

Dusted Roses

Makes 4 roses

125 g/4 oz ivory flower paste
(*see* page 22)
rejuvenator spirit or vodka
dusty-pink tinted lustre powder
50 g/2 oz bright green
ready-to-roll sugarpaste (*see* page 20)
icing sugar, for dusting
green sparkle lustre powder
1 tbsp royal icing

Model a pea-size piece of flower paste into a cone shape. Roll another pea-size piece of flower paste into a ball. Flatten out the ball into a thin petal shape and wrap this round the cone.

Make another petal shape and roll a balling tool round the edges to soften and flute them. Cover the petals with clingfilm and make another 10 petals in the same way.

Press on each petal to attach them round the cone shape, overlapping each petal to form a rosebud. Place in empty egg boxes lined with crumpled foil and fluff out the petals of each to form an open rose. Leave for 8 hours to dry and harden.

Using a fine paintbrush, lightly paint the edges of the rose petals with spirit or vodka and then, with a large stippling brush, dot pink lustre powder over the open rose to give a stippled effect.

Roll out the green sugarpaste on a surface dusted with icing sugar and cut into three leaves with a leaf cutter. Mark on veins with a stamper and then sprinkle with green lustre powder.

Arrange the leaves and roses on the cake, attaching with a dab of royal icing.

Tea Cup Roses

Makes 5 large and 5 small roses and 3 rosebuds

For the cake:
1 large and 1 small shaped cake, covered in white and yellow sugarpaste (see page 20)

To decorate:
450 g/1 lb red flower paste (see page 22)
piping gel
225 g/8 oz strengthened sugarpaste (see page 20)
icing sugar, for dusting
cornflour, for dusting
edible liquid gold paint
1/4 batch royal icing (see page 26)

Roll a pea-size piece of red paste into a ball, then flatten out into a petal with a fatter edge on one side. Make the centre of the rose by curling the petal round into a cone with the fat edge at the base. Make another petal and thin out the top edge. Press the fat edge round the base of the cone and curl the outer edge away. Make another petal and attach a fraction higher than the first, pulling the outer edge away to curl it. Continue adding eight more petals to make the large rose and five for the small rose. Pinch the base together and place the rose in an empty egg box lined with crumpled foil for 24 hours to firm. Make five small and five large roses.

Roll scraps into spiral cones to make three rosebuds and leave in the egg boxes. Fill a small piping bag fitted with a no 2 plain nozzle with piping gel. Pipe 'raindrops' onto the petals and dry for 2 hours.

Make the teacup borders: roll a thin sausage of strengthened sugarpaste on a surface dusted with icing sugar and press into the base of an oval beading mould that has been dusted with cornflour. Press the top over the sugarpaste, then lift this away and tip the string of beaded ovals out onto nonstick baking parchment. Make more strips and leave for 2 hours. Shape a sausage of sugarpaste into handles for the teacups. Paint the border and handles with gold paint and attach with royal icing as shown. Attach the roses with dabs of royal icing.

Orange Blossom Cascade

ε̃

Makes 30 white, 30 light peach, 30 mid-peach and 30 dark peach blossom flowers

700 g/1¹/₂ lb flower paste
(*see* page 22)
light and dark peach paste
food colourings
cornflour, for dusting
¹/₄ batch royal icing (*see* page 26)
120 yellow wired stamens

Leave 175 g/6 oz flower paste white, then divide the remainder into three batches and colour one pale peach, one mid-peach and one dark peach. Wrap each batch of flower paste tightly in clingfilm to keep it flexible.

Roll one batch of flower paste out thinly on a surface dusted with cornflour. Dust the top and base of a silicone blossom mould with cornflour and brush away any excess with a small paintbrush. Make a small ball of flower paste, flatten out between your fingertips and press into the base of the mould. Press the top over the paste then trim away any excess paste around the outside of the mould with a sharp knife. Open the mould and remove the flower.

Place the royal icing in a small piping bag fitted with a no 1 plain nozzle. Thread a stamen through the centre of the flower. Pipe a dot of royal icing on the underside of the flower to secure the wire stamen. Flick the edges of the petals to flute them out, then place the blossom flower in a block of floristry foam to dry for 24 hours. Repeat, making 30 blossoms each in white, light peach, mid-peach and dark peach.

When the flowers are firm enough to handle, carefully remove from the floristry foam and arrange them on the tiered cakes in a cascade, alternating the light and dark colours to give a contrast.

Note: When the cake has been cut, warn your guests to remove the wired flowers before eating.

Springtime Tulips

ℰ

70 assorted flowers and 80 leaves

firm floristry wires, cut into
50 x 8 cm/ 3 inch lengths
175 g/6 oz each yellow, lilac,
pale pink, salmon pink and peach,
350 g/12 oz light green,
225 g/8 oz dark green
and 225 g/8 oz white
ready-to-roll sugarpaste
(see page 20)
icing sugar, for dusting
yellow food paste colouring

Bend the tip of each piece of wire over into a loop. Roll a 2 cm/³/₄ inch long sausage-shaped piece of yellow sugarpaste round the end of the wire, covering the loop, then flatten the end. Make 10 covered wire centres in each colour and stand them in a block of floristry foam to harden for 2 hours.

Roll out the yellow sugarpaste thinly on a surface dusted with icing sugar and cut out six petals using a tulip petal cutter or the template on page 253. Mark the petals with a veining tool, then gently flute the edges with a bone tool. Cover the petals with clingfilm to prevent drying. Lightly dampen the base of a petal with cold boiled water and wrap around the covered wire end. Dampen and wrap another petal around the first, then continue wrapping the petals round, overlapping them. Press the base together, then leave to firm in the floristry foam for 2 hours. Repeat with the remaining colours.

Dust a silicone daffodil mould and press in the white sugarpaste in small pieces. Press out 20 daffodil shapes and leave to dry on nonstick baking parchment for 2 hours. Paint the centres with a little yellow colouring diluted with water.

Make a mound of 125 g/4 oz light green sugarpaste. Shape the remaining light and dark green sugarpaste into a selection of leaves and mark on veins with a veining tool.

Press wired tulips into the paste mound and arrange the daffodils and leaves among them, dampening with a little cold boiled water to stick in place.

Little Red Rosebuds

Makes 120 roses and 108 green leaves

For the cakes:
12 vanilla cupcakes
bought sugar syrup or
125 g/4 oz caster sugar

To decorate:
½ batch cream cheese frosting
350 g/12 oz bright green
ready-to-roll sugarpaste
(*see* page 20)
icing sugar, for dusting
225 g/8 oz bright red
ready-to-roll sugarpaste

If making your own sugar syrup, place the sugar in a saucepan with 150 ml/5 fl oz water and simmer gently for 5 minutes until the sugar dissolves. Cool before using then store in a jar, refrigerated.

Brush the tops of your cupcakes lightly with the syrup. Place the cream cheese frosting in a large piping bag fitted with a star nozzle and pipe swirls on the cakes.

Roll out the green sugarpaste on a surface dusted with icing sugar and, using a small oval cutter, cut into 108 tiny green leaf shapes. Mark each leaf with a sharp knife to make veins, then leave to dry on nonstick baking parchment for 1 hour.

Roll a little of the red sugarpaste into a strip 5 cm/2 inches long by 2 cm/³/₄ inch wide. Wind the strip round to make a simple coiled ribbon rose. Flatten out the edges of some of the strips to make them larger. Make four large and six smaller roses for each cake, totalling 120 roses. Trim the bases so they will sit flat, then leave to firm for 1 hour. Place the roses on the parchment and leave to dry for 1 hour with the leaves.

Arrange nine leaves and the roses on the cakes just before serving.

Pastel Daisies

Makes 12 daisies

500 g/1 lb 2 oz
ready-to-roll sugarpaste
(*see* page 20)
pink and pale green paste
food colourings
cornflour, for dusting
small edible seed pearls
sparkle or glitter powder

Divide the sugarpaste into three batches and colour one pink, one green and leave one white.

Dust a silicone daisy mould with cornflour, then tap away any excess powder. Roll four small balls of sugarpaste each in pink, green and white. Press a ball into the centre of the mould, then press a piece of contrasting sugarpaste on top of this, e.g. a green centre with white daisy leaves. Press the sugarpaste into the mould using your thumbs so that it fills the mould completely.

Cut away any excess sugarpaste, then bend the mould so that the shape falls out. Trim away any edges, then bend the edges of the petals upwards and leave to dry on nonstick baking parchment for 2 hours to firm. Repeat with all the colours, making 12 daisies in all.

Scatter the small seed pearls round the centre of each daisy, then sprinkle over the glitter powder. Carefully lift each daisy onto a buttercream-covered cupcake with a cranked palette knife.

Red Poppies

Makes 12 poppies

225 g/8 oz bright red,
75 g/3 oz black
and 25 g/1 oz bright green
ready-to-roll sugarpaste
(*see* page 20)
icing sugar, for dusting
soft white vegetable
fat, for brushing

Roll out the red sugarpaste on a surface dusted with icing sugar. Using a poppy cutter or a Tudor rose cutter, cut out 12 flower shapes. Mark the flowers with a petal veiner and press the petals upwards to shape them. Leave to dry on crumpled foil, shaped into dips to support the flowers, for 2 hours.

Roll the black sugarpaste into 12 balls and press each one into a silicone raised-flower-centre mould brushed with white vegetable fat. Press to release the centres and leave to dry with the poppies. Alternatively, make the centres by shaping the black sugarpaste into flattened rounds and marking these with a skewer.

Lightly dampen the underside of each black poppy centre with a little cold boiled water and place in the middle of the red petals.

Roll the green sugarpaste into thin sausages and cut into 12 short strips. Bend each green strip to make a curved flower stem and place one on each cupcake. Place the poppy flower on top of the stem just before serving.

Fern Fronds

Makes 14 large and 7 small fern leaves, 20 primroses, 15 acorns, 2 butterflies, 5 large and 3 small wired tan leaves

450 g/1 lb leaf-green,
350 g/12 oz cream,
125 g/4 oz beige,
125 g/4 oz tan and
25 g/1 oz dark brown flower paste
(*see* page 22)
cornflour, for dusting
green medium-gauge floristry wire
edible glue
yellow and brown
paste food colourings
¼ batch royal icing (*see* page 26)

Roll out the green paste on a surface dusted with cornflour. Dust a silicone fern-leaf mould with cornflour. Place a strip of green paste in the mould, clamp on the top and press together. Trim any excess then lift away the top and ease the leaf out. Pinch the base of the leaf together to make a channel then curve the leaf round. Cut some wire the length of the leaf plus 8 cm/ 3 inches. Curve the wire round and stick to the underside of the leaf with edible glue. Leave to dry on nonstick baking parchment for 24 hours. Make 14 large ferns and seven small ones using a smaller mould.

Roll out half the cream paste and stamp out 20 small primroses with a cutter. Press a star tool into the centre of each to make an indentation, dab the centre with yellow colouring and leave for 24 hours. Roll out remaining cream paste and cut out two pairs of butterfly wings using a cutter, or the template on page 250. Fill a small piping bag fitted with a no 1 plain nozzle with brown royal icing and decorate the wings. Leave to dry flat.

Roll the beige paste into 15 small ovals. Loop an 8 cm/3 inch strip of wire and press into each oval. Cover the base of each oval with tan paste and mark on indentations with crumpled foil. Leave the acorns for 24 hours. Roll out remaining tan paste and cut out five large and five small leaves. Mark with a veiner and stick the backs to 8 cm/3 inch strips of wire with edible glue. Leave for 24 hours. Twist the ferns, acorns and primroses in bunches and place round the cake. Make bodies for the butterflies from 25 g/1 oz brown paste rolled into short, fat sausages. Position the wings in place with royal icing, then stick the body in the centre.

Pink Chrysanthemums

Makes 6 pink chrysanthemums

350 g/12 oz flower paste
(*see* page 22)
pink and purple paste food colourings
cornflour, for dusting
1 batch vanilla buttercream
(*see* page 16)

Colour the flower paste light pink with a few dots of paste food colouring. Dust the base of a silicone chrysanthemum mould lightly with cornflour and tip away any excess. Work a small ball of flower paste to make it soft and flexible, then press into the mould. Using a sharp knife, cut across the flower paste to make it level with the top of the mould. Peel the sides of the mould back to release the flower, then carefully place it on nonstick baking parchment to dry flat for 24 hours. Repeat to make five more flowers.

Colour half the buttercream purple and half light pink. Place the purple buttercream in a large piping bag fitted with a basket-weave nozzle. Pipe horizontal lines across, spaced apart by one width of the nozzle, on top of the cake. In the opposite direction, pipe short strips over to form a basket weave.

Place a little of the pink buttercream in a small piping bag fitted with a leaf nozzle. Place the pink flowers on the basket weave icing, then pipe four small pink buttercream leaves round each one.

Place the remaining pink buttercream icing in a large piping bag fitted with a medium star nozzle and pipe a scroll border round the outer edges of the cake, then pipe stars round the sides to finish.

Rose Petal Dream

Makes 1 central rose and 100 petals

cornflour, for dusting
plastic icing sleeve
700 g/1lb¹/₂ oz pink strengthened
sugarpaste (*see* page 20)
rejuvenator spirit or vodka
pink and gold dusting powder
piping gel
dome-shaped cake covered
in buttercream

Dust the inside of the icing sleeve with cornflour. Roll the paste on a surface dusted with cornflour into a 3 cm/1¹/₄ inch sausage, then cut into 130 discs for the petals. Lay the discs inside the sleeve and press on the cover. Press down on each petal to flatten half, leaving a fat edge on one side.

Peel back the sleeve, take one petal and, holding by the fat edge, thin out the top edge with your fingertips. Make the centre of the rose by curling the petal round into a cone with the fat edge at the base. Take another petal and thin out the top edge. Press the fat edge round the base of the cone and curl the outer edge away. Take another petal and attach a fraction higher than the first, pulling the outer edge away to curl it. Continue adding eight more petals. Pinch the base together and place the rose in an empty egg box lined with crumpled foil for 24 hours until firm.

Make 100 petals, pinching the outer edges thinly, then curving downwards to make a tip on the outer edge. Leave to dry on nonstick baking parchment for 8 hours. Dab the edge of each petal with spirit or vodka and dust with pink lustre powder. Dust the central rose with gold lustre powder and place in the middle of the cake. Arrange the petals in a spiral pattern, starting from the centre and fanning outwards. Overlap each petal to give the appearance of a large open rose. Pipe on dots of piping gel to resemble dew or raindrops.

Note: If you have a small icing sleeve, make the petals in two batches.

Flowers & Feathers

Makes 3 feathers, 1 large peony and strings of large and small pearls

225 g/8 oz lilac,
125 g/4 oz dusty pink,
450 g/1 lb white flower paste
(see page 22)
cornflour, for dusting
¼ batch royal icing (see page 26)
cocktail sticks
rejuvenator spirit or vodka
pearl lustre powder

Roll out the lilac paste on a surface dusted with cornflour. Cut into three triangles, 7 cm/3 inches across the base and 15 cm/6 inches high. Pinch each triangle down the centre to make a 'V' shape. Cut into the outer edge of each side with a knife to make feathery fronds. Shape some foil into a 'V' and leave to dry for 24 hours until firm. Make two more feathers.

Roll out the pink paste on a surface dusted with cornflour and, using a peony petal cutter, cut out 20 petals. Keeping the remainder covered with clingfilm, place one petal on a foam block. Using a ball tool, press the centre of the petal to curve; press round the outer edges to frill out. Leave on nonstick baking parchment for 24 hours until firm. Repeat with the remaining pink petals. Repeat with the white paste, making 20 petals. Make five extra petals and curve them round tightly to make the flower centre. Dab the petal bases with royal icing. Starting with the closed centre, build up the petals in an open pattern. Place the white centre on the cake and arrange the pink petals round the base. Attach the feathers as shown with royal icing, supporting them with cocktail sticks.

Dust the inside of a bead mould with cornflour. Mould a piece of paste into a sausage and place across the length of the mould. Close and press together. Open, trim away excess and tip the beads out. Make more beads and leave to dry flat. When dry, paint with spirit and roll in pearl lustre powder. Make more using different sized bead moulds. Attach to your cake with dabs of royal icing.

Note: Remove cocktail sticks before serving.

Frangipani

℮

Makes 12 large and 5 small frangipani flowers and 12 green leaves

450 g/1 lb white and
75 g/3 oz dark green
flower paste (*see* page 22)
cornflour, for dusting
edible glue
rejuvenator spirit or vodka
yellow and pale pink lustre powders
¹/₄ batch royal icing (*see* page 26)

Roll a small ball of flower paste out thinly on a surface dusted with cornflour. Using a frangipani petal cutter or the template on page 251, cut out five petals. Place one petal at a time on a foam pad and, using a bone tool, ease round the sides and tip of the petal to curve the outer edge, leaving the tip flat. Rest the petals on nonstick baking parchment while you make 11 more sets of curved petals.

While the petals are still soft, paint inside the base of five petals with edible glue. Line the petals up in a straight line, then one by one, attach together at the base. Carefully twist to fan out the petals, then pinch the base together. Place the flower in a shaping holder or in an empty egg box lined with crumpled foil and leave to dry for 24 hours. Repeat to make 11 more flowers.

Make five smaller flowers in the same way by using three sets of petals and five buds, using two sets of petals for each bud.

Roll the dark green sugarpaste thinly on a surface dusted with cornflour. Cut out leaves with a leaf cutter and mark with a veiner. Leave to dry for 24 hours.

Brush the centre of each flower or bud lightly with spirit or vodka and dust lightly with yellow lustre powder. Paint the tips with spirit or vodka and very lightly flick on a little pink lustre powder with a soft paintbrush. Arrange the flowers and buds on the cake with the leaves underneath, attaching each with a dab of royal icing.

Strawberry Flowers

Makes 12 flowers and 24 strawberries

12 vanilla cupcakes, covered with
light blue sugarpaste
(*see* page 20)

To decorate:

200 g/7 oz red,
75 g/3 oz green
and 200 g/7 oz white
ready-to-roll sugarpaste
icing sugar, for dusting
1/2 batch royal icing
(*see* page 26)
red and yellow paste food
colourings

To model the red sugarpaste into 24 strawberries, roll a piece of sugarpaste into an oval shape, then pinch the end. Flatten out slightly, then leave to firm for 2 hours on nonstick baking parchment.

Model half the green sugarpaste into 24 small, round leafy tops for the strawberries, dampen lightly with cold boiled water, then press them onto the red shapes. Roll out the remaining green sugarpaste on a surface dusted with icing sugar and cut out 24 leaves with a leaf cutter. Pinch the centres and leave to dry on the parchment for 2 hours. Using scraps, roll a thin sausage and cut into 24 short stalks. Curve each stalk and leave to dry with the leaves.

Roll out the white sugarpaste on a surface dusted with icing sugar and stamp out 12 small, open daisies using a daisy cutter. Shape the daisies to open out the petals and leave to dry for 2 hours.

Arrange one daisy, two strawberries, two leaves and a stalk on each cake and attach with dabs of royal icing. Colour half the remaining royal icing red and half yellow. Place in small paper icing bags fitted with a no 1 plain nozzle and pipe yellow dots on the strawberries. Pipe red dots on the flowers and round the sides of the cakes as shown.

Open Rose

Makes 3 large open roses and 3 rosebuds

long yellow stamens
medium gauge floristry wires
350 g/12 oz pink
and 175 g/6 oz green
flower paste (*see* page 22)
cornflour, for dusting
rejuvenator spirit or vodka
green lustre powder

Bind a bunch of the yellow stamens together with an 8 cm/3 inch long strip of wire. Roll out the pink flower paste on a surface dusted with cornflour. Using a large five-petal cutter, cut out five sets of petals, place one set on a foam pad, keeping the remaining paste and petals covered with clingfilm. Press firmly round the outer edges of each petal with a ball tool to frill up. Turn the petal over and repeat to give ruffled edges. Repeat with the remaining four sets of petals.

Dampen the centre of each set of petals with cold boiled water. Thread the wired stamens through the petal, with the yellow centres in the middle. Thread the remaining petals onto the wire, behind the first petal, fluffing them out. Stand the rose to dry in a circlet of crumpled foil for 24 hours. Repeat to make two more open roses.

To make the rosebuds, roll a small pea-size cone of paste and attach to an 8 cm/3 inch piece of wire. Roll and cut out five sets of petals, dampen the centres and thread these over the wire to the cone. Wrap the petals round the cone, pressing together to close them up. Make three rosebuds and leave for 24 hours.

Roll out the green paste and cut out six sets of leaves with a leaf cutter. Mark with a veiner, then leave to dry for 24 hours on nonstick baking parchment.

Brush the undersides of the roses and rosebuds with spirit or vodka and brush the outsides of the rosebuds with green lustre powder before arranging the flowers.

Spring Daffodils

Makes 2 large daffodils, 6 buds and 6 green leaves

125 g/4 oz yellow,
225 g/8 oz orange,
125 g/4 oz green
and 175 g/6 oz white
ready-to-roll sugarpaste
(*see* page 20)
icing sugar, for dusting

Roll out the yellow sugarpaste on a surface dusted with icing sugar and, using a large petal cutter, stamp out 12 petals. Mould a little orange paste into a strip and cut one side with a fluted wheel cutter or pasta wheel. Cut into two short strips and roll each round into a cone. Dampen the underside of each petal with cold boiled water and arrange on the cake in an overlapping pattern. Dampen the base of the cone and press into the middle of the petals.

Roll out the green sugarpaste thinly on a surface dusted with icing sugar. Cut into long leaf shapes with a leaf cutter or sharp knife, then mark on veins with the point of a sharp knife. Dampen the underside of each leaf with cold boiled water and stick onto the cake as shown.

Using scraps, make small orange sausages of sugarpaste. Mould yellow scraps into small, flat cones and wrap these round the sausages to make small buds.

Make a twisted border for the cake. Roll out a long, thin sausage of white sugarpaste to a length long enough to go round the base of the cake. Repeat with a long thin sausage of orange, then loosely twist the two together. Place round the base of the cake and dampen the join with cold boiled water. Dampen the small buds and arrange on the cake.

Ribbons, Pearls Roses

Makes 3 large bows, large round pearls, small oval pearls and 16 small moulded roses

cornflour, for dusting
450 g/1 lb flower paste (*see* page 22)
rejuvenator spirit or vodka
pearl, green, pearlised pink, blue and yellow metallic lustre powders
450 g/ 1lb strengthened sugarpaste (*see* page 20)
icing sugar, for dusting
50 g/2 oz each light and dark green flower paste

Dust the inside of a large resin bead mould with cornflour. Roll a piece of flower paste into a sausage and place across the length of one side of the mould. Close and press together. Open, trim away excess paste and lift the beads out. Make more strips of beads and leave to dry flat on nonstick baking parchment. When dry, paint with spirit or vodka and roll in pearl lustre powder and some in green. Make more pearls with small oval-shaped bead moulds.

Knead the strengthened sugarpaste, then roll out on a surface dusted with icing sugar and cut into thick strips, about 10 cm/4 inches wide. Use a ribbon roller to cut the strips, then place on the cake. Bend two strips over to the centre to form loops, dampen lightly with cold boiled water and stick onto the cake. Cut a 'V' shape into the ends of four flat strips and position these under the loops of the bow. Take a short strip, dampen lightly, scrunch together, then position over the join in the centre. Brush the bow with spirit or vodka, then dust with pearlised pink lustre powder. Repeat to make two more bows.

Make roses by pressing flower paste into small silicone rose moulds dusted with cornflour. Peel away the mould and leave to dry for 8 hours. Cut out 10 light and dark green leaves with a leaf cutter and leave to dry with the roses. Paint the roses with spirit or vodka and dust with coloured metallic dusting powders. Arrange the roses and leaves on the cake with the ribbons and pearls.

Sunshine Daisies

Makes 5 daisies with green leaves

soft white vegetable
fat, for brushing
125 g/ 4 oz leaf-green and
225 g/8 oz buttercup yellow
flower paste (*see* page 22)
cornflour, for dusting

Have ready a silicone chrysanthemum or large petal daisy mould and lightly brush with white vegetable fat into all the corners.

Roll five tiny balls of green flower paste and keep aside covered with clingfilm. Knead a small ball of yellow paste until soft and flexible and press into the mould, using your thumb so that the paste fills the mould completely. Cut away any excess, then bend the mould so that the petal shape falls out.

Place this first set of curved petals round the green ball and set aside covered with clingfilm. Make four more sets of curved petals in the mould and dampen the centre of each one lightly with cold boiled water. Stick the sets of petals round the green central ball, curling the petals outwards, and leave to dry on nonstick baking parchment for 24 hours. Repeat to make four more flowers.

Roll out the remaining green flower paste on a surface dusted with cornflour and stamp out 10 ivy leaves using an ivy leaf cutter. Mark on veins using a veiner embossing mould or the tip of a sharp knife. Curl the edges of each leaf lightly with your fingertips, then leave to dry on parchment for 24 hours.

Arrange the green leaves underneath the daisies to make a contrast.

Open Poppies

ℰ

Makes 8 poppies

medium gauge floristry wire, cut
into 8 lengths 15 cm/6 inches
225 g/8 oz dark blue,
225 g/8 oz bright orange and
125 g/4 oz green flower paste
(*see* page 22)
cornflour, for dusting

Bend the end of each wire to make a tiny loop. Smooth a small ball of blue flower paste over the loop to cover it, then press the paste between your fingertips to flatten. Place the wire in a block of floristry foam to harden for 3 hours. Make four blue centres, then repeat with the remaining wires and orange paste.

Roll the remaining blue flower paste thinly on a surface dusted with cornflour and cut out eight petals using a large open petal cutter, or mark round the template on page 253 and cut out with a sharp knife. Place each petal on a sponge pad and press with a ball tool round the edges to curve it. Dampen the base of a petal lightly with cold boiled water and wrap this round the stamen centre on the wire. Attach another petal, leaving this a little more open. Continue until you have wrapped eight petals onto the wire. Repeat, making four blue flowers and four orange flowers. Place the flowers on a drying rack or in open cones made from doubled pieces of crumpled foil and leave to harden for 24 hours.

Roll out the green paste on a surface dusted with cornflour and cut into eight large leaves. Press the leaves with a veining mat and leave to dry on nonstick baking parchment for 24 hours.

Arrange the poppies and the leaves on the cake, alternating the colours.

Calla Lillies

ℭ

**Makes 10 lilies,
6 blue flowers and
12 green leaves**

75 g/3 oz light yellow,
75 g/3 oz dark yellow,
225 g/8 oz white,
175 g/6 oz light blue
and 125 g/4 oz green
flower paste (see page 22)
medium gauge floristry wires,
cut into 8 cm/3 inch lengths
cornflour, for dusting
125 g/4 oz white ready-to-roll
sugarpaste (see page 20)

Roll the light yellow flower paste into 10 thin sausage shapes and thread each piece onto the end of a floristry wire. Repeat with the dark yellow paste, making six sausages on wires for stamens for the blue flowers. Snip the end of each dark yellow sausage into three with tiny scissors. Leave all to dry in a block of floristry foam for 8 hours.

Roll out the white flower paste on a surface dusted with cornflour and cut out ten 8 cm/3 inch squares. Roll the edge of each square with a ball tool to make a curve, then wrap a white petal round a yellow centre, pressing the end together to form an open lily. Place in the floristry foam and leave to dry for 8 hours. Make 10 lilies.

Dust a silicone fancy veined petal mould with cornflour and flick away any excess. Press a blue ball into the mould and press on the top piece. Trim away any excess, then remove the top mould and release the petal from the base. Make 36 petals. Mould six petals round the base of the open wired centres. Flick the petals outward and leave to dry upside down on nonstick baking parchment for 8 hours.

Roll out the green flower paste and cut out 12 large leaves with a leaf cutter, mark on veins with a quilting tool, pinch the ends together and leave to dry.

Make a ball with the sugarpaste and then flatten down into a mound shape. Assemble the wired flowers and leaves by pressing into the sugarpaste mound.

Animal
Friends

There is nothing quite like a child's reaction to miniature animals on top of a cake made just for them. This section offers options to satisfy children's imaginations by creating colourful fantasies involving Wise Owls, Farm Animals and Sleeping Dragons, among others. Pick and choose which animals you want to create so you can tell the story you want. Any way you cut it, whoever you're making the cake for will remember it for years to come!

Little Teddy

Makes 1 bear

50 g/2 oz light brown,
25 g/1 oz black
and 25 g/1 oz pink
ready-to-roll sugarpaste
cocktail stick
red decorative ribbon

Roll 15 g/^{1}/$_2$ oz light brown paste into a thick sausage and cut into four. Roll into two arms and two legs. Roll 15 g/^{1}/$_2$ oz paste into a round for the body and a smaller round for the head. Make ears and muzzle from scraps.

Flatten the body slightly at the base and top, and place on each white sugarpaste-covered cupcake. Shape the arms and stick in place with a little cold boiled water. Flatten out the feet, then stick the legs in place. Flatten out the head slightly, then place on a cocktail stick and secure to the body. Stick on the ears and muzzle.

Mark on stitching with a quilting tool, then mark on a mouth and details on the feet with a fine skewer. Make one large and two small balls of black paste for the eyes and nose and stick in place on the face.

Roll out the pink paste and stamp out five tiny discs for petals. Dampen with a little cold boiled water. Press the petals together, then place between the bear's paws. Place on the cake.

Note: Don't forget to tell your guests that the bear contains a cocktail stick. Alternatively, if you are worried about using cocktail sticks with children, affix the head to the body with a dampening of cold boiled water or a dab of royal icing.

Jungle Animal Playtime

Makes 3 blocks, a lion and a monkey

For the blocks:

3 x 5 cm/2 inch cubes vanilla
sponge cake
$1/4$ batch vanilla buttercream
(*see* page 16)
125 g/4 oz each of blue, green,
yellow, green and orange
ready-to-roll sugarpaste
(*see* page 20)
icing sugar, for dusting

For the animals:

125 g/4 oz light tan,
25 g/1 oz dark brown,
15 g/$1/2$ oz black,
15 g/$1/2$ oz white,
175 g/3 oz light brown
and 50 g/2 oz mid-brown
ready-to-roll sugarpaste

Coat the cubes with buttercream. Roll out the coloured sugarpastes on a surface dusted with icing sugar, then cut into squares large enough to cover the sides of the cubes. Press a square onto each side of the cube in contrasting colours and smooth on. Stamp out letters in contrasting colours and stick to the sides with cold boiled water.

To make the lion, roll 25 g/1 oz ball of light tan sugarpaste into an oval, 2.5 cm/1 inch long, then flatten the top slightly. Shape a sausage and cut in half for the arms; repeat and make two legs. Mark claws on the ends with a blunt knife. Roll 25 g/1 oz ball of sugarpaste to make the head. Roll four small tan balls, two for ears and two for the muzzle. Roll two tiny balls of white sugarpaste for the eyes, then make three tiny black rounds. Stick two in the eyes' centres and one in the centre for the nose. Roll a strip of dark brown sugarpaste and snip one edge to make the mane. Stick the pieces together.

To make the monkey, roll 25 g/1 oz mid-brown sugarpaste into a ball for the body and a 15 g/$1/2$ oz ball for the head. Roll a sausage and cut in half for the arms. Repeat for the legs; press out the ends of each and shape to make paws. Roll two small rounds and stick on the head for ears. Stick the head and arms onto the body. Decorate the front of the body, ears, eye area and muzzle with light brown sugarpaste and mark on a nose. Roll two tiny balls of white sugarpaste for the eyes; roll two tiny black rounds and stick in the eyes' centres. Press the eyes onto the light brown rounds.

Ladybird Garden

Makes 12

½ batch royal icing (*see* page 26)
green, black, yellow and red paste
food colourings
225 g/8 oz ready-to-roll
sugarpaste (*see* page 20)
icing sugar, for dusting

Colour half the royal icing green, then a quarter black and a quarter yellow. Colour 50 g/2 oz sugarpaste red, 25 g/1 oz black and leave the rest white.

Roll the red sugarpaste into 12 tiny balls, then make each one into an oval. Flatten the oval slightly, then mark a line down the back with the back of a knife. Roll the black sugarpaste into small rounds and press one onto the front of each ladybird. Leave to dry on nonstick baking parchment for 3 hours.

Roll the white sugarpaste out thinly on a surface dusted with icing sugar and stamp out 48 small daises with a daisy cutter. Mark indentations down each petal, then curve the petals round. Press one set of petals inside another and leave the 24 flowers to dry on the parchment for 3 hours.

Place the green royal icing in a small piping bag fitted with a leaf nozzle and pipe four green leaves onto each cupcake. Place the yellow royal icing in a small piping bag fitted with a no 1 plain nozzle. Place two daisies onto the green leaves and pipe on yellow dotted centres.

Pipe two yellow dots for eyes onto each ladybird. Place the black royal icing in a small piping bag fitted with a no 1 plain nozzle and pipe black dots onto the red part. Place a ladybird onto each cupcake with the flowers.

Golden Elephants

Makes 2 elephants standing on a round plaque

225 g/8 oz strengthened
sugarpaste (see page 20)
cornflour, for dusting
450 g/1 lb flower paste
(see page 22)
edible glue
cocktail sticks
edible gold lustre spray

Knead the sugarpaste into a ball and roll out on a surface dusted with cornflour. Cut out a disc 14 cm/5^1/$_2$ inches in diameter and 1.5 cm/^{1}/$_2$ inch thick. Mark a pattern round the sides with an embossing tool. Model a small drum from scraps, 2.5 cm/1 inch in diameter and 2 cm/^{3}/$_4$ inch thick. Roll strips into thin sausages to make a top and base border, then mark scraps into triangles. Stick these on the drum with glue, then stick the drum in the centre of the disc. Leave to dry on nonstick baking parchment for 24 hours.

Divide the flower paste in half. Using one half, divide into one third for the head and ears and two thirds for the body. For the head, remove 50 g/2 oz for the ears and mould the remaining paste into an oval. Roll one end of the oval into a sausage for the trunk. Make a cut under the trunk with a knife for the mouth. Mark on eyes with a fine skewer, then curve the trunk as shown. Insert a cocktail stick in the base of the head. Mould two flat ears, curving the edges outwards. Mould the body piece into an oblong. Bend the oblong over at each end and cut each end in two to make the legs. Mould the legs, broadening the base of each to make a flat foot, then mark on nails with a skewer. Dab each foot with edible glue and position on the drum and the plaque as shown. Repeat to make the other elephant and position both as shown. Leave heads, ears and bodies to dry for 24 hours.

Make strips of beads using sugarpaste scraps in a small bead mould and leave to dry. Stick onto the bodies. Press the heads on the cocktail sticks into the bodies, securing with glue, then glue on the ears. Model two scraps into thin sausages for tails. Stick on as shown. Spray two or three coats of gold spray all over the models. **Note:** Remove the cocktail sticks before serving.

Sleeping Dragon

Makes 1 dragon

125 g/4 oz bright green,
15 g/¹⁄₂ oz white
25 g/1 oz dark blue,
and 15 g/¹⁄₂ oz black
ready-to-roll sugarpaste
(*see* page 20)
drinking straw
confectioner's glaze (optional)

For the body and tail, roll 50 g/2 oz green sugarpaste into a tapering sausage, about 15 cm/6 inches long. Divide 50 g/2 oz green sugarpaste into two thirds and one third. Use the smaller amount to make two small sausages for the back legs. Use the larger amount to make two larger sausages for the front legs.

Mould 25 g/1 oz green sugarpaste into an oval for the head. Flatten the front and use the tip of a knife to mark a mouth, then make two nostrils with the end of a paintbrush. Make two tiny white sugarpaste ovals for the eyes. Bend the green sugarpaste back to make eyelids and press the eyes onto the head, bending the eyelids over each eye as shown.

Roll out the blue sugarpaste to a long, thin, tapering strip, 15 cm/6 inches long and cut one side into 'V' shapes.

Place the body of the dragon on the cake, dampen the underside of the head with cold boiled water and press onto the body. Bend the two front legs over, dampen and position near the head. Dampen the two back legs and position. Mark scales all over the body with the end of a drinking straw. Dampen the plain edge of the blue strip and press onto the dragon's back.

Curve the dragon's tail round into position as shown. Roll white scraps of sugarpaste into horns and claws, dampen lightly and position as shown. Roll tiny scraps of black sugarpaste into thin sausages and stick one onto each eye. For a shiny finish, lightly paint the green body parts with confectioner's glaze.

Farm Animals

Makes 3 sheep, 3 pigs and 3 cows

For the cakes:

12 chocolate cupcakes
3 tbsp apricot glaze

To decorate:

50 g/2 oz green,
75 g/3 oz light pink,
175 g/6 oz white,
25 g/1 oz cream,
25 g/1 oz brown,
25 g/1 oz dark pink,
15 g/½ oz black,
25 g/1 oz turquoise blue
and 25 g/1 oz dark blue
ready-to-roll sugarpaste
(*see* page 20)
icing sugar, for dusting

Spread the cupcakes with apricot glaze. Roll the green sugarpaste into small balls on a surface dusted with icing sugar. Flatten each into a leaf and stick four leaves on each cake.

To make the sheep, roll a little pink paste into 75 g/3 oz white sugarpaste and roll into three ovals. Roll scraps of white paste into thin sausages, then curl each sausage into a spiral and stick to the back of the sheep's body with cold boiled water. Roll a small ball of cream sugarpaste, stick to the front of the sheep and flatten out. Make four small hooves from brown sugarpaste. Place the sheep and hooves on the leaves.

To make the pigs, roll the light pink sugarpaste into three balls. Model two scraps for ears and four trotters. Stick on the ears and trotters. Model a dark pink snout, stick onto the front and mark two nostrils with a fine skewer. Place the pigs on the leaves.

To make the cows, roll the remaining white sugarpaste into three ovals. Roll four small sausages for legs and stick to the body. Model a dark pink nose, stick on the front of the cow and mark on nostrils. Model pink ears, black spots and hooves and stick on. Make small brown horns and stick onto the head. Place the cows on the leaves.

Model small, round black eyes with curved tips and stick onto the animals, then place a white dot of sugarpaste on each one. Stamp out small hearts, dots and daisies with the remaining sugarpaste and use to decorate the cakes.

Bedtime Friends

Makes 1 rabbit, 1 moon and 1 bear

175 g/6 oz white,
25 g/1 oz pink,
15 g/^{1}/$_2$ black,
15 g/^{1}/$_2$ oz orange,
15 g/^{1}/$_2$ oz green,
50 g/2 oz yellow
65 g/2^1/$_2$ oz light brown
and 15 g/^{1}/$_2$ oz dark brown
modelling paste (*see* page 24)
cocktail sticks
food colouring pens
edible gold lustre paint

To make the rabbit, roll a 40 g/1^1/$_2$ oz ball of white paste for the body and a 25 g/1 oz ball for the head. Model two ears and stick to the head with cold boiled water. Roll four sausages for the arms and legs and flatten out the paws. Model ears, face, belly and feet patches from pink paste, then stick on as shown. Make two small black balls for eyes and stick on. Press on two small white balls from scraps for the cheeks. Position the body, head and limbs on the cake and stick in place. Mark on the tummy button with a skewer. Roll the orange paste into carrots, making green tops, and stick in place.

To make the moon, roll the yellow paste into a curved shape with pointed ends. Model an eye, nose and lips and stick in place. Roll 25 g/1 oz white paste out thinly and wrap around the top to form a hat, fluting out the broad end and making a ball at the tip. Insert a cocktail stick halfway into the base of the moon, leaving one half exposed. Leave to dry flat on nonstick baking parchment for 8 hours, then decorate with a colouring pen and gold paint.

To make the bear, roll 15 g/^{1}/$_2$ oz light brown paste into a thick sausage and cut into four. Roll into two arms and two legs. Roll 25 g/1 oz paste into an oval for the body and 15 g/^{1}/$_2$ oz into a round for the head. Make ears and a muzzle from scraps. Flatten the body slightly at the base and place on the cake. Shape the arms and legs and stick in place. Flatten out the head slightly, then place on a cocktail stick and secure to the body. Stick on the ears and muzzle. Make small black balls for the eyes and nose and stick in place. Decorate the ears and paws with dark brown paste. Mark on stitching with a quilting tool, then make a bow from scraps and finish with gold paint. **Note:** Remove cocktail sticks before serving.

Coral Reef

Makes 1 castle, 1 angel fish, 1 goldfish, rocks and coral

175 g/6 oz grey,
75 g/3 oz orange,
25 g/1 oz black,
75 g/3 oz white,
50 g/2 oz purple,
25 g/1 oz red and
15 g/½ oz green
modelling paste (*see* page 24)

Flatten 125 g/6 oz of the grey paste into an oblong. Model one end of the oblong at a right angle to make the castle, with an archway underneath. Make ridges to represent turrets with the side of a modelling tool handle. Mark on brickwork with a skewer and leave to dry flat on nonstick baking parchment for 8 hours. With the remaining grey paste, model two rocks and leave to dry flat.

To make the clown fish, mould 50 g/2 oz orange oblong and flatten one end into a tail. Roll out a little black and white paste and cut into strips. Dampen the strips and decorate the fish as shown. Make two eyes with black and white circles and stick in place. Model three fins, place one on top and one on either side and position as shown. Roll most of the remaining 25 g/1 oz orange paste into five short sausages, make a dip in the centre of each one with a bone tool then make the edges thinner. Leave to dry.

To make the angel fish, mould the remaining white paste into a flat triangular shape then model into a head, tail and fins as shown. Roll black paste, cut into strips, dampen and decorate as shown. Make eyes. Leave to dry flat.

Twist some orange scraps with some purple paste together into short sausages, make a dip in the centre of each one with a bone tool, then make the edges thinner. Leave to dry. Model longer twisted purple and green oblong pieces as shown and leave to dry flat. Roll some purple, red and green pastes into flat discs and decorate as shown. To complete, press the pieces into the top of a buttercream-covered cake.

Bow Tie Bear

Makes 1 bear and appliqué decorations

100 g/3¹/₂ oz ivory modelling paste
(*see* page 24)
350 g/12 oz pink,
15 g/¹/₂ oz black,
25 g/1 oz white and
350 g/12 oz cream
ready-to-roll sugarpaste
(*see* page 20)
cocktail stick
icing sugar, for dusting

To make the bear, roll 40 g/1¹/₂ oz ivory modelling paste into a thick sausage and cut into four. Roll into two arms and two legs. Roll 25 g/1 oz paste into an oval for the body and 15 g/¹/₂ oz into a round for the head. Make ears from two balls of scraps and make a dip in each one. Make small balls of ivory paste and inset these with tiny pink balls. Flatten the body slightly at the base and place on the cake. Shape the arms and legs, mark on ridges with a fine skewer and stick in place with a little cold boiled water. Model the head so that there is a pointed end at the front, then place on a cocktail stick and stick onto the body. Stick on the ears.

Decorate the face with a skewer, colour tiny scraps black and make three small black balls for the eyes and nose and stick in place. Model a pink heart, a bow and small discs and buttons. Decorate the ears, paws and feet with pink and white sugarpaste discs; stick the heart, buttons and bow tie in place.

Roll out the pink and cream sugarpaste thinly on a surface dusted with icing sugar and stamp out a selection of discs, daisies, flowers and hearts in different sizes. Stick the larger designs round the cake and then build up layers using the smaller ones in a different colour. Stick pink daises with small white centres round the bear.

Note: Remove the cocktail stick before serving.

Spring Chickens

Makes a mother, father, 2 baby chicks and a selection of flowers

For the cake:

1 x 20 cm/8 inch round cake covered in mint green sugarpaste (see page 20)

To decorate:

175 g/6 oz yellow,
225 g/8 oz orange,
50 g/2 oz mint green,
125 g/4 oz dark green,
50 g/2 oz white,
75 g/3 oz blue,
75 g/3 oz red
and 25 g/1 oz purple
ready-to-roll sugarpaste
icing sugar, for dusting
black food colouring pen

Model two small chicks in 50 g/2 oz each yellow sugarpaste, then roll out the remainder on a surface dusted with icing sugar and cut out eight yellow daffodil flowers with cutters. Model 125 g/4 oz orange sugarpaste into an oval for the mother chicken, then stamp out six orange butterflies. Mix the mint green sugarpaste with the remaining orange paste and model the father chicken. Model beaks with orange and red sugarpaste and stick in place with cold boiled water.

Place balls of the dark green sugarpaste in an icing or garlic press and push out into long strands for the grass. Stick in small piles on top and around the sides of the cake with cold boiled water as shown.

Roll out the white sugarpaste and stamp out 16 small daisies; make yellow dots for the centres. Roll out the blue paste and stamp out 54 tiny blossom flowers. Roll out a scrap of red paste and stamp out 20 tiny blossoms. Stick the daffodils, blossoms and daisies onto the cake as shown. Use the remaining pastes to decorate the feathers and beaks of the chickens. Paint dots on the faces for eyes with the black pen.

Hungry Rabbit

Makes 1 rabbit and carrots

125 g/4 oz grey,
15 g/¹/₂ oz pink,
25 g/1 oz white,
15 g/¹/₂ oz black,
25 g/1 oz orange and
15 g/¹/₂ oz green modelling
paste (*see* page 24)

To make the rabbit, roll 40 g/1¹/₂ oz ball of grey paste for the body and 25 g/1 oz ball for the head. Roll two small sausages for the arms and flatten out for the paws. Roll two more sausage shapes for legs and feet and press the ends flat. Model two flat grey ears and decorate the ears and feet by modelling and sticking on a little pink sugarpaste as shown, then stick the ears on the head with a little cold boiled water.

Make a small pink nose and stick into position. Roll two small white balls and two small black balls for the eyes and stick in place on the head. Decorate the face with discs of white paste; make a white bib shape for the front with the remaining white paste. Make two tiny white squares from scraps and press onto the face for teeth. Position the head, arms and feet on the body and stick in place. Decorate the feet with tiny pink patches and mark on claws with a skewer.

Roll the orange paste into carrots, make flattened green tops from the green paste and stick in place. Mark indentations on the carrots and tops with a fine skewer. Place the rabbit on the cake and put a carrot between his paws. Scatter the remaining carrots round the rabbit.

Pretty Kitty

Makes 12 kittens with red hearts

75 g/3 oz red,
350 g/12 oz orange,
50 g/2 oz white
and 25 g/1 oz pink
ready-to-roll sugarpaste (*see* page 20)
icing sugar, for dusting
black food colouring pen

Roll out the red sugarpaste thinly on a surface dusted with icing sugar and stamp out 12 hearts with a small heart cutter. Spread the hearts out to dry on nonstick baking parchment for 4 hours.

Roll 15 g/¹/₂ oz of orange sugarpaste into a fat sausage, then cut into four pieces. Roll for the arms and legs, pinching one end of each piece to make a thin end. Model 25 g/1 oz into an oval for the body. Model 15 g/1 oz into a ball for the head, then pinch a corner on each side to make two ears.

Roll scraps of white paste to make a figure of eight shape, dampen and stick onto the face with a little cold boiled water. Roll a pink scrap for the nose and stick in place, then model two tiny pink triangles and stick on to decorate the ears. Roll two tiny white discs and stick on for the eyes. Roll a tiny scrap of red sugarpaste into a ball and stick on for the mouth. Leave the head to dry on the parchment for 1 hour.

Decorate the head with a black food colouring pen. Draw on eyebrows, then colour in the eyes, leaving a white rim and white dots showing. Draw on eyelashes, then black dots on the white muzzle.

Place the body on a pink sugarpaste-covered cupcake and stick the arms and legs in place. Stick the head onto the body, then stick a red heart in front of the cat. Repeat to make 11 more kittens.

Dapper Penguin

Makes 1 penguin

50 g/2 oz black,
25 g/1 oz white,
15 g/¹/₂ oz orange
and 15 g/¹/₂ oz red modelling
paste (*see page 24*)

To make a penguin, roll 15 g/¹/₂ oz black paste into an oblong and flatten out one end. Roll 10 g/¹/₄ oz black paste into a small sausage 6 cm/2¹/₂ inches long and drape it over the oblong, pinching the ends to make two flippers. Roll 10 g/¹/₄ oz into a small black ball for the head. Roll out the white paste thinly and cut out a small teardrop shape. Stick the white shape onto the penguin's front with a little cold boiled water. Roll a small oblong strip and stick to the underside of the head, bringing up the two ends with a dip in the middle, as shown.

Roll out the orange paste thickly and cut out two small discs for the feet. Mark dips on with a skewer for the webbing. Dampen the base of the body and place on the feet. Dampen the head and place onto the body. Make a small cone shape with orange sugarpaste to form a beak. Stick the beak onto the head, then finish the face by rolling two tiny black dots and sticking these on for the eyes.

Roll a strip of red modelling paste thinly and cut into a scarf long enough to go round the penguin's body. Cut tassels in each end of the scarf with a sharp knife and drape the scarf round the penguin.

Wise Owl

Makes 1 owl with 7 pumpkins

1 mini Swiss roll or cake bar
1 tbsp vanilla buttercream
(*see* page 16)
225 g/8 oz ivory,
125 g/4 oz orange,
10 g/¼ oz black and
50 g/2 oz green
ready-to-roll sugarpaste
(*see* page 20)
icing sugar, for dusting
drinking straw
orange paste food colouring
confectioner's glaze
liquid edible gold food colouring

Cut the cake into two pieces, 5 cm/2 inches and 7 cm/2½ inches deep, then trim the top and bottom edges to make them domed. Spread the pieces with buttercream and place the smaller piece on top of the larger one.

Roll out the ivory sugarpaste thickly on a surface dusted with icing sugar into a square large enough to cover the cake pieces. Drape the sugarpaste over and press in place, pinching in between the top and bottom pieces of cake to make an indentation for the owl's head. Model two ears out at either side of the head by pinching between your thumb and fingertips. Mark the owl's body with the end of a drinking straw to make feathers. Roll scraps of ivory sugarpaste into two flat ovals to make the wings. Dampen the underside of each wing and press in place, lifting the wing up again.

Roll two scraps of orange sugarpaste into flattened balls for the eyes. Make black sugarpaste into two tiny strips and stick onto the eyes. Paint details with orange paste colouring as shown and leave to dry for 1 hour. Make a small beak with orange scraps and leave to dry. Paint the eyes and beak with confectioner's glaze, then leave to dry for 4 hours.

Roll the remaining orange sugarpaste into seven small balls and flatten each one slightly. Mark on indentations with a skewer. Roll the green sugarpaste into thin strips. Dampen the top of each pumpkin with cold boiled water and press the green strips on to decorate. Dampen the backs of the eyes and beak and press in place. Make eyebrows from scraps and press over the eyes. Paint the owl's feathers on with gold colouring.

Valentine Dalmatian

Makes 1 dalmation with red heart

75 g/3 oz white,
25 g/1 oz black
and 25 g/1 oz red
ready-to-roll sugarpaste
(*see* page 20)
icing sugar, for dusting

Roll 25 g/1 oz white sugarpaste into a fat sausage, then bend this in half, so that the long ends touch each other. Model each end to flatten out slightly to form the front feet. Repeat with another fat sausage, bending in half again. Dampen the back of the front legs with a little cold boiled water and stick to the front legs. Put a little pressure on the legs so that they will stand upright.

Model 25 g/1 oz white sugarpaste into an oval. Press the front to flatten, then pinch in the middle to shape the face as shown. Model two round cheeks, then make a ridge with a skewer to make the mouth as shown. Flatten the underside of the head, dampen lightly, then press onto the body.

Roll half the black sugarpaste into two long, thin strips and shape into ears with rounded ends. Dampen lightly, then stick the ears to either side of the head. Roll two small, black balls for the eyes and a larger one for the nose. Roll two smaller white balls and two tiny black balls and stick onto the eyes. Stick the eyes and nose onto the body. Roll scraps into small black dots, stick one under the nose and the rest on the body.

Roll the red sugarpaste out thinly on a surface dusted with icing sugar and cut out a tiny heart. Use scraps to make a flat tongue shape and stick in place under the mouth. Stick the heart in front of the dog's paws to finish.

Monkey Island

Makes 2 monkeys and 2 palm trees

125 g/4 oz yellow,
50 g/2 oz red,
50 g/2 oz green,
225 g/8 oz brown and
125 g/4 oz beige marzipan
50 g/2 oz white
ready-to-roll sugarpaste
(see page 20)
icing sugar, for dusting
tube black piping icing
2 thin liquorice sticks
cocktail sticks

Model the yellow marzipan into bananas and open banana skins. Use white sugarpaste to fashion pieces of 'peeled' banana to stick onto open banana skins. Roll red and yellow marzipan thinly on a surface lightly dusted with icing sugar and stamp out blossoms with a flower cutter. Roll thin strips of green marzipan and drape round the cake.

Make a large and a small brown monkey. Roll round body pieces and long, thin sausages for arms, legs and tails. Make beige ovals and stick to the body parts. Make brown and beige heads, beige ears and beige mouths and cut across to open them. Roll small white sugarpaste balls for eyes and red strips for tongues. Pipe small black dots on the eyes and mark nostrils on the faces with a fine skewer. Assemble as shown, then place on the cake with the bananas.

Roll the remaining brown marzipan into long, thin strips and wrap around the liquorice sticks to make tree trunks. Bend and place on the cake, securing with cocktail sticks. Make green marzipan palm leaves, snipping the edges with scissors, and press onto the trees. Roll long, thin green sausages for vines and red and yellow scraps to stamp out thin daisies. Arrange all as shown.

Note: Remove cocktail sticks before serving.

At The Zoo

Makes 1 elephant, 1 giraffe, 1 zebra and a fence

125 g/4 oz grey,
225 g/8 oz white,
225 g/8 oz beige,
25 g/1 oz brown and
125 g/4 oz black modelling
paste (see page 24)

For the elephant, roll two grey balls each 25 g/1 oz for the head and body. Roll a 25 g/1 oz sausage and cut into four lengths, flattening out the end of each for feet. Model two flat ears and a trunk from the remaining paste. Roll white discs for the ears and nails and stick on with cold boiled water. Stick all the pieces together, then mark the trunk and eyes with a fine skewer.

For the giraffe, model 25 g/1 oz of white paste into a cone and flatten the top. Roll 40 g/1¹/2 oz beige paste into a long sausage, cut into four and stick a length either side of the body for the back legs and the other two at the front. Roll four small balls of white paste and stick to the ends of the legs. Roll 10 g/¹/4 oz beige paste into a ball. Make a smaller ball of white paste, stick to the beige ball, smooth into an elongated shape for the head, then stick onto the body. Model two beige discs for ears, place two smaller white discs on top, pinch each ear together, then stick to either side of the head. Roll brown paste into two horns and stick to the head. Roll the remaining brown paste into small balls and stick to the body to decorate.

For the zebra, model the body, legs and head as for the giraffe, using black instead of white for the hooves and muzzle. Stick the head onto the body. Model two white discs for ears and place two smaller black discs on top, pinch each ear together, then stick to either side of the head. Roll a white strip and place a black tip on the end for the tail. Roll a small sausage of black paste and stick to the head for the mane. Roll black paste into short, thin strips, dampen and stick to the body for the stripes. Roll the remaining beige paste into oblong strips, dry for 3 hours then make a fence.

Yellow Duckling

Makes 12 ducklings and small decorations

450 g/1 lb yellow
and 75 g/3 oz orange
ready-to-roll sugarpaste
(*see* page 20)
icing sugar, for dusting
tube black piping icing
sparkle powder

Model 15 g/¹⁄₂ oz yellow sugapaste into an oval. Roll 10 g/¹⁄₄ oz into a ball and flatten the base. Roll 15 g/¹⁄₂ oz into two balls and flatten each one out into an oval. Pinch the end of the oval together to make a wing tip and point this upwards. Stick the head and wings onto the duck's body with a little cold boiled water and leave to firm on nonstick baking parchment for 2 hours. Make 11 more ducks.

Roll out the orange sugarpaste thinly on a surface dusted with icing sugar. Cut into a thin strip, then cut diagonally to make a diamond shape. Cut the diamond shape in half and stick both flat sides to the duck's head to make the beak. Make 11 more and stick to the remaining ducks.

To finish, pipe on two small black dots on each duck for eyes. Place the ducks in the middle of buttercream-covered cupcakes and sprinkle over sparkle powder just before serving. Roll out yellow scraps and cut out small duck shapes to decorate the cupcakes.

Grazing Sheep

Makes 3 sheep on a green base

50 g/2 oz peach,
50 g /2 oz white,
15 g/¹/₂ oz brown,
75 g/3 oz ivory and
25 g/1 oz dark yellow
modelling paste (*see* page 24)
50 g/2 oz leaf-green sugarpaste
(*see* page 20)
icing sugar, for dusting

Divide three quarters of the peach modelling paste into three and roll each one into a ball. Roll each ball into an oval, then flatten one end for the head. Mark on a ridge and nostrils for the nose with a skewer. Make two dips in each head with a small bone tool. Roll tiny white balls, dampen lightly with a little cold boiled water, then place in the dips for the eyes. Roll small brown balls and stick these onto the eyes. Model peach scraps into flat ears and stick either side of the head.

Divide three quarters of the ivory paste into three and roll into ovals. Dampen the underside of each head and stick onto the oval bodies. Place the remaining ivory paste into a garlic press and press out to make strands of fleece. Position the fleece over the ears and tails and press on lightly.

Roll out the green sugarpaste on a surface lightly dusted with icing sugar and mould into a triangle. Mark on a grass pattern with the tines of a fork.

For the flowers, roll the remaining white modelling paste into balls, flatten out and place five together. Mark to indent the petals with a small bone tool, then roll a small yellow centre and stick in place.

Place the sheep and daisies on the green grass.

Bunnies

Makes 12 decorated rabbits

500 g/1 lb 2 oz beige,
25 g/1 oz pink,
25 g/1 oz yellow,
25 g/1 oz lilac,
25 g/1 oz white and
10 g/¹/₄ oz black
ready-to-roll sugarpaste
(*see* page 20)
black food colouring pen
white piping icing tube
iced gem flower sweets

Use 40 g/1¹/₂ oz beige sugarpaste for each rabbit. To make a rabbit, roll a small ball of beige sugarpaste for the body and a smaller round for the head. Roll two small sausages for the arms. Roll two more sausage shapes for legs and feet and press the ends flat. Stick all the pieces together with cold boiled water.

Model two flat beige ears and decorate the ears and feet by modelling pink sugarpaste patches, then stick in place to the head with a little cold boiled water as shown. Make 11 more rabbits, decorating three more with pink sugarpaste, four with yellow and four with lilac. Leave the rabbits to dry flat on their backs on nonstick baking parchment for 4 hours until firm.

Roll two tiny discs of white sugarpaste for each rabbit and stick closely together on their faces. Make small pink noses and stick into position. Roll two small black balls each for eyes and stick in place on the heads. Pipe tiny white teeth under the white discs. Using the black pen, draw on whiskers and tiny black dots on faces as shown. Pipe a dot of icing onto the back of each gem flower sweet and place in the rabbits' paws.

Honey Bear

Makes 1 bear with tree and honeypots

225 g/8 oz yellow,
125 g/4 oz brown,
15 g/¹/₂ oz red,
10 g/¹/₄ oz white and
50 g/2 oz green modelling
paste (*see* page 24)
icing sugar, for dusting
cocktail stick
white food colouring pen
1 small blue striped candle
very fine gauge floristry wire

Use 125 g/4 oz yellow paste to make the bear. Roll a 50 g/2 oz ball for the body, then flatten out to a teardrop. Roll two small sausages for arms, flatten out the ends slightly and model into hands with thumbs. Roll two small sausages for legs and feet and position as shown. Model 25 g/1 oz into a head, shaping the front to make a snout; mark stitching onto the face and lower body with a quilting tool. Shape two tiny ears and press in place. Use brown paste to make eyebrows, small dots for the eyes, a triangular shaped nose and mouth, and press into place.

Roll the red paste out on a surface dusted with icing sugar and wrap around the bear to make a T-shirt with sleeves on each arm. Stick the head in position by dampening underneath with cold boiled water, then securing with a cocktail stick.

Roll two small balls of brown paste, then flatten out to make the honey pots. Model yellow scraps and stick on top of the pots for the honey. Write 'Honey' round the sides with the pen and insert the candle in one pot. Twist six tiny balls of yellow and brown paste together to make a stripy effect. Make tiny white wings and stick in place, then place each bee on a curled strip of wire. To make the tree, knead the remaining brown and yellow paste together and shape into a trunk with three branches. Mark on bark. Roll out the green paste and cut into small leaves with a cutter or knife. Dampen the branches and stick the leaves on, overlapping them. Leave everything to dry flat on nonstick baking parchment for 8 hours.

Note: Remove the cocktail stick and wires before serving.

Mice With Cheese

Makes 3 mice

125 g/4 oz grey,
15 g/$^1/_2$ oz pink,
10 g/$^1/_4$ oz black and
25 g/1 oz yellow modelling paste
(*see* page 24)

Use 25 g/1 oz grey paste for each mouse's head and body. Using 10 g/$^1/_4$ oz, model a teardrop-shaped head, turning the point upwards. Make two more heads, then flatten six tiny balls into ears for each mouse. Model a body with 15 g/$^1/_2$ oz modelling paste for each mouse. Mark on a tummy button with a fine skewer.

For the reclining mouse, flatten the body out and cut into two legs. Model grey scraps into arms, feet and a tail. Dampen the underside of each head and tail with cold boiled water and stick to the body. Stick on the feet. Roll pale pink paste into six tiny balls, dampen and stick onto the ears to decorate. Roll tiny pink balls for the mouths and stick in place. Use a small bone tool to make impressions for the eye sockets. Roll small black balls for the eyes and noses and stick in place.

Model the yellow paste into three rounds for pieces of cheese and mark holes in each one with a small bone tool. Stick the cheese onto each mouse's chest, then stick the arms over the cheese to hold it in place.

Model grey scraps into tails and stick in position, curling some of them round.

Happy Frog

Makes 1 frog

40 g/1^1/$_2$ oz green,
15 g/^{1}/$_2$ oz cream,
15 g/^{1}/$_2$ oz black,
10 g/^{1}/$_4$ oz pink and
15 g/^{1}/$_2$ oz red
ready-to-roll sugarpaste
(*see* page 20)

Roll 25 g/1 oz green sugarpaste into a ball. Make the remaining green sugarpaste into four small squares. Mark each square with a sharp knife to make hands and feet.

Roll the cream sugarpaste into two balls and press onto the top of the head. Roll two small black balls and press onto the eyes, flattening them as you press them on. Make a thin black sausage for the mouth and press in place. Roll two small pink balls and press in place for the cheeks.

Roll the red sugarpaste into a ball and flatten out. Make a black bow tie with scraps and place on top of the red piece. Dampen the underside of the head with a little cold boiled water and stick the head onto the red body. Stick the hands and feet in place.

People

Just about everybody enjoys receiving a homemade and hand-decorated cake, no matter the occasion. This section offers options to really bring your cake to life, with a person to suit any occasion, whether it be a wedding, christening or just a fun party. Try putting the Knight and his Maiden on an anniversary cake, or the Princess and the Frog on a little girl's birthday cake. Baby's Bathtime is perfect for anyone's first birthday cake!

Singing Angel

🎵

Makes 1 angel

65 g/2¹/₂ oz light pink,
15 g/¹/₂ oz flesh-coloured,
40 g/1¹/₂ oz purple,
25 g/1 oz lilac and
10 g/¹/₄ oz white modelling
paste (*see* page 24)
rejuvenator spirit or vodka
yellow, pink pearl and lilac
pearl lustre powders
tubes white, black, pink and
yellow writing icing

Model 50 g/2 oz pink paste into a cone and flatten the top and wider base. Stand the cone flat on nonstick baking parchment. Model two arms with 15 g/¹/₂ oz paste and press onto the body. Model a small head and hands with 15 g/¹/₂ oz flesh-coloured paste. Stick the head on the top of the cone body and the hands onto the arms.

Roll 12 small balls of purple paste and 16 small lilac balls. Roll a lilac ball and pull out one end to make a small oblong with rounded ends. Make seven more oblongs and arrange them in a rounded shape for the top of the wing, overlapping the oblongs and pressing them together. Repeat to make the top of the other wing. Shape the purple paste as before for the base of the wing and repeat, overlapping and shaping into two wings. Leave to dry for 24 hours. Roll the remaining purple paste into two thin strips and place round the neck and base of the angel. Model a book from white paste, mark pages and spine and leave to dry. Brush with spirit and dust the 'cover' with yellow lustre powder.

Brush the body and arms with spirit, then dust with pink lustre powder. Brush the wings and the two bands on the body with spirit and dust with lilac lustre powder. Pipe two dots of white icing onto the face for eyes, then pipe a black dot on each one and a round pink mouth. Pipe on coils of yellow icing for hair. Pipe a pink squiggly border round the base and neck of the angel. Stick the wings and book in place with dabs of white icing.

Knight ❧ Fair Maiden

Makes 1 knight and
1 maiden

125 g/4 oz pale pink,
25 g/1 oz white,
50 g/2 oz magenta pink,
125 g/4 oz burgundy,
25 g/1 oz yellow and
175 g/6 oz grey modelling
paste (*see* page 24)
3 plastic cake pop sticks
icing sugar, for dusting
black food colouring pen
cocktail stick
rejuvenator spirit or vodka
silver lustre powder

For the maiden, roll a large ball of pale pink paste into a teardrop shape, flatten the top and base and insert a cake pop stick through the centre. Shape a 15 g/¹/₂ oz ball of paste for the head and model the centre to form a nose. Press on two tiny white discs for eyes and mark on a mouth with a skewer. Place the head on the stick. Model two arms with hands and press onto either side of the body. Model a small magenta pink paste cone for the hat, then roll the rest out on a surface dusted with icing sugar. Drape the paste down the front of the model to form the underskirt, fluting out the hem; trim across the top for the bodice. Roll out the burgundy paste and use a little to trim the hat. Drape the remaining paste round the figure to make a dress with sleeves, crossing over at the top, leaving the underskirt and hands showing. Flute up the edges. Press the yellow paste through a garlic press to make hair and press round the head. Stick on the hat with cold boiled water and draw black dots on the eyes. Stamp out blossoms with a small cutter from white scraps and arrange in her hands.

For the knight, roll two sausages of grey paste round two cake pop sticks, leaving the tops exposed. Model the feet. Roll a 75 g/3 oz grey oval for the body. Roll two arms, model the hands and stick to the body. Roll a 15 g/¹/₂ oz pale pink ball for the head and cover with grey paste, leaving an eye gap. Roll a pale pink ball for the nose and two white balls for the eyes, stick on and draw on black dots. Stick the head on a cocktail stick and place on the body. Press the legs into the body. Roll grey scraps and decorate the armour as shown. Make a burgundy plume for the helmet. Leave to dry flat for 24 hours before standing upright. Brush the models with spirit and dust with lustre powder.

Note: Remove all sticks before serving.

Nativity Scene

Makes 1 Virgin Mary, 1 shepherd, 1 angel and 1 Jesus in a manger

225 g/8 oz white,
50 g/2 oz pink,
25 g/1 oz blue,
50 g/2 oz yellow,
25 g/1 oz green and
75 g/3 oz brown modelling paste
(*see* page 24)
cocktail sticks
liquid gold food colouring
tubes black and white writing icing
red food colouring pen

Roll three 40 g/1 1/2 oz pieces white paste into cone shapes, then flatten the top and base of each. Roll 15 g/1/2 oz pink paste into a ball and press onto each body, securing with a cocktail stick. For Mary, roll two blue arms and a strip of blue paste to go round the body. Trim to make a coat, then press the arms in place. Push 15 g/1/2 oz yellow paste through a garlic press to make hair and press in place on her head. Model a white veil to cover her hair.

For the shepherd, roll a green strip and press onto the front of the body. Roll two brown arms and trim a strip to make a brown coat. Roll a brown crook. Roll out white paste to make a beard and moustache and press onto the face. Make a brown head covering and trim with a green band.

For the angel, model two white arms and stick to the body with cocktail sticks. Roll white paste and cut into two wings with fluted edges. Make a circlet for a halo. Paint the wings and halo with gold and leave to dry on nonstick baking parchment for 2 hours. Roll 15 g/1/2 oz yellow paste out thinly and press into small pleats for hair.

For the baby Jesus, shape 25 g/1 oz brown paste into an oblong manger. Roll the remaining 25 g/1 oz yellow paste out thinly and cut into an oblong with jagged edges for the hay. Roll a tiny pink ball and wrap this round in white paste for the swaddling. Decorate all the faces with tiny pink balls for noses and piped black dots for eyes and mark on mouths with the red pen. Model pink hands and stick to the arms. Place the crook in the shepherd's hand and stick on the angel's wings and halo with dabs of white icing.
Note: Remove the cocktail sticks before serving.

Little Princess

ℰ

Makes 1 princess

50 g/2 oz ivory ready-to-roll
sugarpaste (*see* page 20)
gold metallic balls
125 g/4 oz peach,
75 g/3 oz light pink,
25 g/1 oz dark pink and
25 g/1 oz brown modelling
paste (*see* page 24)
icing sugar, for dusting
drinking straw
plastic cake pop stick
black food colouring pen
tube white writing icing

For the cushion, roll the sugarpaste into a ball, then flatten the top and base to make a round shape. Mark on criss-cross lines to make a diamond pattern. Push gold balls into the points where the diamonds meet.

Model two long thin peach sausages for legs, then make tiny light pink shoes and press onto the feet. Drape the legs on the cushion, crossing the feet over. Roll a 25 g/1 oz peach oval for the body and place on the back of the cushion. Roll a ball of light pink paste out to a thin disc on a surface dusted with icing sugar. Roll the edge of the disc with a frilling tool, then cut out tiny circles around the edge with the end of a drinking straw. Dampen the body with cold boiled water and stick on the dress, frilling up the skirt and pressing the bodice in place. Roll two thin sausages for arms, model the hands and stick in place as shown.

Model a round for the head with 25 g/1 oz peach paste and mark on a mouth with a skewer. Push the plastic stick into the body and cushion, then place the head on top of the stick, leaving a gap to make a long neck. Model peach scraps round the stick to make a thin neck. Roll brown paste out thinly and cut into a circle for the hair. Dampen the head and stick the hair on loosely. Model small brown sausages and stick on either side of the head. Roll thin pink strips to make the ribbons and stick in place. Make a dark pink coronet and stick on top of the head. Roll a small peach nose and stick in place, then mark on eyes with the pen. Pipe on a necklace and straps and decorate the dress with dots white icing.

Note: Remove the stick before serving.

Footballer

Makes 1 footballer

15 g/^{1}/$_2$ oz black,
50 g/2 oz peach,
15 g/^{1}/$_2$ oz white and
40 g/1^1/$_2$ oz red
ready-to-roll sugarpaste
(*see* page 20)
2 tbsp brown buttercream
(*see* page 16)
tubes white, yellow, red and
black writing icing

Model three quarters of the black paste into two rounds for the boots. For the legs roll two small sausages of peach sugarpaste and stick the boots on the end of each with cold boiled water. Roll three quarters of the white sugarpaste into two balls, flatten out and stick onto the top of the legs to make the shorts.

Roll a 25 g/1 oz red ball and flatten one end to make the body. Stick the body onto the shorts. Roll two small red sausages for arms and stick onto the body. Roll two peach balls and stick onto the arms for hands. Model two tiny red squares and stick onto the top of the body for the collar.

Roll a 25 g/1 oz ball of peach sugarpaste for the head. Stick the head onto the body, securing with a cocktail stick. Model two ears and a nose from peach paste and stick on. Roll two tiny white balls and stick on for eyes. Roll a small white ball for the football, stick on tiny black sugarpaste dots then press onto one of the boots. Lay the footballer on his back and leave to firm on nonstick baking parchment for 8 hours.

Place the buttercream in a small piping bag fitted with a small star nozzle and pipe brown hair on the head. Pipe a white number on the jersey and a yellow stripe on one arm. Pipe on a red mouth and black eye dots to finish.

Note: Don't forget to tell your guests that the footballer contains a cocktail stick. Alternatively, if you are worried about using cocktail sticks with children, affix the head to the body with a dampening of cold boiled water or a dab of royal icing.

Bride & Groom

Makes 1 bride and 1 groom

125 g/4 oz peach,
75 g/3 oz white,
25 g/1 oz yellow,
25 g/1 oz pale green,
25 g/1 oz pink,
75 g/3 oz black and
15 g/^{1}/$_2$ oz brown modelling
paste (*see* page 24)
2 plastic cake pop sticks
icing sugar, for dusting
black food colouring pen

For the bride, shape 25 g/1 oz peach paste into a thin cone around the cake pop stick, leaving 3 cm/1^1/$_4$ inches uncovered at each end. Mould the top to make the bride's shoulders and taper the top inwards to the neck. Roll 50 g/2 oz white paste into a square and cut a 'V' shape in one side. Wrap the bodice around the top of the body. Roll two thin arms from peach paste and stick on as shown. Wrap the skirt round the body, overlapping the front. Stand the body upright on the stick. Mould a 25 g/1 oz peach ball for the head, press to indent the front as shown and place on the stick. Roll the yellow paste out thinly on a surface dusted with icing sugar and cut into strands for hair. Press the hair onto the head and curl up the ends. Roll pale green paste into a thin sausage and make a circlet and place on the head. Roll remaining green paste out and cut out small leaves and stalks. Roll pink paste into thin strips and roll up to make tiny roses. Stick the leaves, roses and stalks to the bride's hands with cold boiled water. Decorate the circlet with roses and leaves. Attach ribbons made from white scraps under the bouquet.

For the groom, roll a 25 g/1 oz white cone of paste and mould 3 cm/1^1/$_4$ inches down around the other stick. Roll black paste into two thin sausages for legs and feet and wrap round the stick under the white body, leaving 3 cm/1^1/$_4$ inches exposed. Model two sausages for arms, and a black waistcoat and jacket. Wrap the waistcoat/jacket round the white part, then press on the arms. Model two pink hands and stick to the arms. Model a bow tie and stick to the shirt. Mould a head as for the bride and place on the stick. Roll brown paste for hair and press in place, marking with a knife. Mark the faces with the black pen. **Note:** Remove the sticks before serving.

New Family

c

Makes a mother, father and baby, a sofa, 2 small tables and a rug

50 g/2 oz ivory,
225 g/8 oz red,
350 g/12 oz light brown,
50 g/2 oz dark brown,
125 g/4 oz white,
40 g/1¹/₂ oz lilac,
50 g/2 oz pink and
15 g/¹/₂ oz yellow strengthened
sugapaste (*see* page 20)
brown paste food colouring

To make the rug, roll 50 g/2 oz ivory paste to an oblong and make thin cuts into each end. Paint stripes on the rug with brown colouring and leave to dry flat on nonstick baking parchment for 24 hours.

To make the sofa, model a thick oblong of red paste for the seat and another for the back and press the two together. Roll small red sausages for the arms, press on each end, mark details with a skewer and leave to dry for 24 hours.

Model the light brown paste into an oblong for the coffee table; make four short legs and press onto the table. Leave to dry upside down. Make a light brown disc for the small table and a circular base and leg. Press together and leave to dry upside down. Model two dark brown pots and two white mats and leave to dry.

Roll the lilac paste into two sausages for legs, cross them over and place on the sofa. Roll a 25 g/1 oz white cone for the father's jumper and press onto the legs. Roll a white sausage for his arm and press onto the jumper. Roll a 15 g/¹/₂ oz ball for the head and press in place. Roll two light brown legs for the mother and place on the sofa. Model a 40 g/1¹/₂ oz body from pink paste and press onto the legs, thinning the edge for a hem for the skirt. Model two pink sausages for arms. Roll a 15 g/¹/₂ oz ball for the head and press in place. Roll a small, light brown ball for the baby's head, then model a white blanket and wrap this round. Place the baby on the mother's lap. Model hands and feet for the father. Make brown hair for the father and yellow hair for the mother and press in place. Model white balls for eyes and stick in place, then paint on features with brown colouring.

Cricket Crazy

ℰ

Makes 1 cricketer and decorations

For the cake base:

1 x 20 cm/8 inch, round
Madeira cake, covered with
buttercream and green sugarpaste

To decorate:

400 g/14 oz ready-to-roll
sugarpaste (see page 20)
black, brown, pink, red
and tan paste food colourings
icing sugar, for dusting
cocktail stick
small amount royal icing
(see page 26)
small tube writing icing
green ribbon trim

Colour 100 g/3½ oz sugarpaste black, roll out on a surface dusted with icing sugar and cut out enough 2 cm/¾ inch squares for your message. Leave to dry on nonstick baking parchment. Colour 75 g/3 oz sugarpaste brown and model the trophy as shown, using bits of white to make the labels. Leave to dry as above.

Using 175 g/6 oz white sugarpaste, make the cricketer – take half, roll into a sausage about 15 cm/6 inches long, flatten, trim, fold in half and hang over the side of the cake, attaching with cold boiled water. Use the rest to make the body, arms and feet and attach them with a little water. Colour 40 g/1½ oz sugarpaste pink and make the hands and head from small balls, pressing features into them with a knife or modelling tool. Attach the head with a cocktail stick.

Colour the remaining sugarpaste red and tan to make a ball, bat, stumps and hair, attaching them all with cold boiled water. With black paste colouring mixed with a little water, paint the trophy label and features on the face. Paint a little pink colouring on his cheeks and nails. With royal icing and a small writing tube, pipe markings on the cricket ball and letters on the black tiles. Stick these and the trophy onto the cake with dots of royal icing. Trim with a green ribbon around the board.

Note: Remove the cocktail stick before serving.

Pirate

Makes 1 pirate with treasure chest and parrot

75 g/3 oz red,
25 g/1 oz black,
40 g/1¹/₂ oz pink,
25 g/1 oz white,
25 g/1 oz brown,
25 g/1 oz yellow,
15 g/¹/₂ oz orange and
50 g/2 oz tan
ready-to-roll sugarpaste
(*see* page 20)
icing sugar, for dusting
cocktail stick
black food colouring pen
pirate flag

To make the body, roll a 40 g/1¹/₂ oz cone of red sugarpaste and flatten the top and base. Roll black paste out thinly on a surface dusted with icing sugar and cut out a waistcoat. Press the pieces onto the body. Roll two red sausages for arms and press onto the body. Roll two small balls for hands and press onto the arms. Roll a 25 g/1 oz pink ball for the head and flatten slightly, then place on the body, securing with a cocktail stick. Roll a tiny pink ball for the nose and press in place. Roll two white sausages for legs. Cut black paste into thin strips and press the strips onto the legs. Lay the legs flat and press the red body on top of them. Roll two brown balls for feet, then press onto the legs. Roll yellow sugarpaste out to a circle, then press onto the head for hair. Roll a thin sausage of red sugarpaste and press round the hair. Roll tiny yellow balls of sugarpaste and press onto the waistcoat. Make a black eye patch, press in place and decorate the face with the black pen.

To make the parrot, roll a small triangular piece of red sugarpaste and shape into a bird body. Model an orange beak and cut a mouth with a knife. Roll small white balls for the eye and press on. Mark the eyes with the black pen.

To make the treasure chest, shape a tan sugarpaste oblong and mark with a knife to represent wood. Cut in to create the open lid. Trim with strips of brown sugarpaste; make a small lock and mark with a fine skewer. Roll small yellow balls and flatten them for gold coins and place in the chest. Thread the flag onto a wooden skewer and press into the cake.
Note: Remove the cocktail stick before serving.

Baby's Bathtime

Makes 1 baby in bath with boat, duck, frog and sponge

For the cake:

20 cm/8 inch Madeira cake or cake bar
3 tbsp sieved apricot glaze

To decorate:

350 g/12 oz blue,
75 g/3 oz pink,
15 g/^{1}/$_2$ oz red,
350 g/12 oz white,
50 g/2 oz yellow,
10 g/^{1}/$_4$ oz dark blue,
10 g/^{1}/$_4$ oz brown and
15 g/^{1}/$_2$ oz green
ready-to-roll sugarpaste
(*see* page 20)
icing sugar, for dusting
cocktail stick
silver edible metallic liquid paint
black and red food colouring pens

Cut the cake so that it tapers to 13 cm/5 inches at the base and 17 cm/6^1/$_2$ inches at the top, by about 7 cm/2^1/$_2$ inches wide. Cut away the edges to make them round. Brush with apricot glaze. Roll out the 350 g/12 oz blue sugarpaste on a surface dusted with icing sugar to a square large enough to cover the cake. Lift the icing over the cake and smooth down over the top and sides. Roll blue scraps into a thin sausage and press round the top edge of the bath.

Roll the pink sugarpaste into two balls, keeping two small scraps aside. Flatten one ball and place in the bath. Place a cocktail stick in the mound and press the other ball on top for the head. Model two pink ears and a button nose and press in place.

Model a small red boat, decorate with white scraps, then model a yellow curl and press onto the baby's head. Model a yellow duck and press on a dark blue base. Model a yellow sponge and mark small circles on; make a string from twisted strips of brown sugarpaste. Model a green frog with white eyes. Leave the boat, duck, sponge and frog on nonstick baking parchment. Roll a white strip into a long thin sausage and place round the base of the bath. Roll another thin sausage and bend the end over. Wrap a small scrap round the top and leave to dry for 4 hours.

Roll white sugarpaste into large and smaller balls and fill the bath with them. Place the duck and boat in the bath. Paint the tap and bath trim with silver paint. Draw details on the baby's face, duck and frog with the pens.
Note: remove the cocktail stick before serving.

Princess ❧ The Frog

Makes 1 princess with frog

175 g/6 oz flesh-coloured,
15 g/¹/₂ oz green,
10 g/¹/₄ oz white,
350 g/12 oz shell-pink
and 25 g/1 oz brown modelling
paste (*see* page 24)
cocktail sticks
icing sugar, for dusting
edible glue
liquid edible gold paint
green, red and brown food
colouring pens

Roll a 25 g/1 oz flesh-coloured ball for the head and model the face, then place the head on a cocktail stick. Roll the remaining flesh paste into a cone for the upper body and shape into a neck and bust, tapering down into a waist. Place a cocktail stick in the waist part, leaving half exposed. Press the head into the body part. Roll two sausages for arms, model flat hands and bend the arms upwards. Place the princess on her back on nonstick baking parchment. Support the head and arms with crumpled foil and leave to dry for 8 hours.

Model the green paste into an oval and model a small frog, marking on a mouth with a knife. Press two tiny white balls on for eyes. Leave to dry for 8 hours.

Roll a thick pink sausage for the legs and bend round to a 'U' shape. Place on the cake, then press the upper body on the cocktail stick onto the legs. Roll out the pink paste thinly to an oblong on a surface dusted with icing sugar and flute the edges with a frilling tool. Wrap the pink paste across and round the body, trimming to fit with scissors. Roll two thin panels for the train at the back and frill the edges. Stick one on top of the other onto the back of the body with edible glue. Model a belt and bow and press round the waist. Stick the arms on with glue.

Model the brown paste into a long oval for the hair and press onto the head. Make a twist; press on round the back of the head. Paint the join gold for a hair clasp. Mark on facial features and decorate the frog with the pens. **Note:** remove the cocktail sticks before serving.

Elfin Baby

ℰ

Makes 1 baby, oak leaves, ferns, red and brown mushrooms and a pumpkin

50 g/2 oz sage-green,
50 g/2 oz light brown,
50 g/2 oz peach,
50 g/2 oz light green,
40 g/1¹/₂ oz pink,
50 g/2 oz dark brown,
40 g/1¹/₂ oz red,
50 g/2 oz white,
15 g/¹/₂ oz orange and
15 g/¹/₂ oz black
ready-to-roll sugarpaste
(see page 20)
icing sugar, for dusting
cocktail stick
black food colouring pen

Roll the sage-green sugarpaste out on a surface dusted with icing sugar and cut out four oak leaves using a cutter or the template on page 253. Mark with a knife and curl up the edges. Repea to make four light brown leaves.

Roll a 15 g/¹/₂ oz ball of peach sugarpaste for the baby's head and place on a cocktail stick. Roll a 40 g/1¹/₂ oz cone and cut the tapering end into two, shaping the feet and legs. Stick the head on the cocktail stick into the body and lay on the cake on a green leaf. Model 10 g/¹/₄ oz light green sugarpaste into a conical hat and stick on the head. Roll pink sugarpaste into two small sausages and make two arms, then press onto the body. Roll small peach balls for hands and press onto the arms. Roll remaining pink sugarpaste out thinly and cut into small squares for the baby's clothes. Drape over the figure in layers, fluting up the edges. Make a small button nose and press onto the face, mark on a mouth with a skewer and draw on eyes with the black pen.

Model the dark brown sugarpaste into a log. Mark with a knife to represent bark and place on the cake. Model red and white sugarpaste and light brown and white sugarpaste into toadstools and mushrooms and place round the cake. Model an orange pumpkin and make a light green top from scraps. Roll the remaining light green sugarpaste and cut out ferns with a cutter and place round the cake with the remaining leaves. Make two ladybirds by rolling red scraps into two small ovals and pressing a tiny ball of black sugarpaste on each for the head. Mark on a cut in the back for the wings and draw on black dots with the pen. **Note:** Remove the cocktail stick before serving, or omit entirely, using cold boiled water to affix the head.

Birthday Tea

ℰ

Makes 1 table, a cake, sandwiches, a tea set, 2 square presents and 1 child

350 g/12 oz white,
125 g/4 oz red,
25 g/1 oz light blue,
125 g/4 oz pink,
50 g/2 oz peach,
15 g/^{1}/$_2$ oz yellow and
15 g/^{1}/$_2$ oz light green
ready-to-roll sugarpaste
(see page 20)
light brown, blue and black
paste food colourings
1 giant cupcake or muffin
2 tbsp vanilla buttercream
(see page 16)
icing sugar, for dusting
cocktail sticks

Cover a 15 cm/6 inch round cake board with 125 g/4 oz white sugarpaste and mark with a knife to represent wooden flooring. Blend a little light brown colouring with water, brush over the board and leave to dry for 4 hours.

Trim the top of the cupcake flat, spread with buttercream and place on the board. Roll out 125 g/4 oz white sugarpaste on a surface dusted with icing sugar to a 23 cm/9 inch disc. Drape loosely over the cupcake and trim the edges with scissors so that the cloth just touches the floor. Using a fine paintbrush with blue paste colouring, paint a repeating pattern on the cloth.

Model a 2.5 cm/1 inch cube from red sugarpaste and another from light blue. Make thin strips and bows from white sugarpaste and stick round the cubes with cold boiled water. Stack the cubes at one side of the table. Make a 50 g/2 oz cone with pink sugarpaste and flute out the base. Roll peach balls for feet and place on the present. Stick the pink cone on the feet, then roll sausages for arms and stick to the table. Make peach hands and stick to the arms. Roll a 25 g/1 oz peach ball for the head and stick onto the body, securing with a cocktail stick. Roll out the yellow sugarpaste and shape for the hair, then stick onto the head and mark with a knife. Make a red conical hat with a pink tassel and secure to the head with a cocktail stick. Make a button nose and stick on the face, then paint on eyes with black colouring. Model a layer cake from small discs of red and white sugarpaste as shown and cut two slices out. Model plates and cups and saucers and paint the tea brown with colouring. Make sandwiches from pink and white scraps. Model a green milk jug with a pink top.
Note: Remove the cocktail sticks before serving.

Seasonal & Celebration

Sugarcraft can easily be used to make any cake suit any event, whether you want to celebrate seasonal festivities or a special occasion. From Christmas to graduation, this section offers a multitude of projects to make your cake the centrepiece of any party. The Smiley Snowman is a cute complement to any winter-themed cake, and the New Home will delight at a housewarming party.

Santa With His Presents

Makes 1 Santa with presents and a tree

50 g/2 oz red,
25 g/1 oz black,
50 g/2 oz flesh-coloured,
50 g/2 oz green,
10 g/¹⁄₄ oz blue and
10 g/¹⁄₄ oz lilac
ready-to-roll sugarpaste
(*see* page 20)
cocktail stick
tube white writing icing
black food colouring pen
white sparkle powder

Roll half the red sugarpaste into a cone shape for Santa's body, then flatten out the base and top. Roll a small sausage of red sugarpaste and cut in half. Model into two arms and press onto either side of the body. Roll two small black balls for the feet and press in place. Make a black belt from scraps and press round the body. Roll two small flesh-coloured balls for hands and press onto the arms, then make a trim for the belt from flesh scraps.

Roll 25 g/1 oz flesh-coloured paste into a ball and stick onto the body, securing with a cocktail stick. Make a small ball for the nose and press in place. Model a red hat and stick onto the head.

To make the Christmas tree, roll the green paste into a cone shape and flatten the base. Using small scissors, snip into the cone, making small 'V' shapes to make the foliage. Model the blue and lilac sugarpaste into small cubes for the presents.

Using the tube of white icing, pipe dots onto Santa's face to make a beard and moustache, then pipe a trim round the hat and a bobble on top. Draw on the eyes with the black pen. Pipe ribbons on the presents, then sprinkle the presents and the tree with sparkle powder to finish.

Note: Remove the cocktail stick before serving.

First Birthday Bear

Makes 1 large bear, 1 toy rabbit, presents, a cake and balloons

75 g/3 oz light pink,
125 g/4 oz white,
10 g/¼ oz black,
25 g/1 oz dark pink,
10 g/¼ oz lilac
50 g/2 oz blue and
15 g/½ oz light brown
modelling paste (*see* page 24)
cocktail stick
1 candle and holder
icing sugar, for dusting
firm gauge floristry wire

To make the bear, roll 15 g/½ oz light pink paste into a thick sausage and cut into four. Roll into two arms and two legs. Roll 25 g/1 oz paste into an oval for the body and 15 g/½ oz into a round for the head; make ears from scraps. Flatten the body slightly at the base, and place on the cake. Shape the arms and legs and press in place. Flatten out the head slightly, then place on a cocktail stick and secure to the body. Press on the ears. Make a small muzzle, press on and mark with a skewer. Roll small black balls for eyes and nose and press in place. Decorate the feet with white paste. Roll out dark pink and lilac paste and cut out small blossoms with a cutter. Roll tiny white centres, then press onto the bear's ear as shown.

To make the rabbit, model 25 g/1 oz white paste into an oblong for the body, making one end fatter. Roll a 15 g/½ oz ball for the head. Roll a thin sausage and cut into six pieces for arms, legs and ears. Place the rabbit's body underneath the bear's arm, then stick two thin legs to the body. Stick two thin arms over the bear's arm. Press on the head, then press the last two thin strips on for ears, flattening out the ends.

Model blue and pink paste into small cubes and decorate with thin strips of white paste, making small bows on top. Make a cake by rolling thin discs of white, dark pink and light brown paste, then layering them as shown. Press the candle and holder into the cake. To make balloons, roll blue and white scraps out on a surface dusted with icing sugar and cut out small 2 cm/¾ inch discs. Thread onto 10 cm/4 inch lengths of wire and leave to dry flat on nonstick baking parchment for 4 hours. Press into the cake and arrange round the bear. **Note:** Remove the cocktail stick and wires before serving.

Babies' Bootees

Makes 2 bootees

225 g/8 oz white modelling paste
(*see* page 24)
icing sugar, for dusting
¼ batch royal icing

Roll the paste out thinly on a surface dusted with icing sugar. Trace round the template patterns on page 251 and cut out two sole shapes, two toe pieces and two backs.

Lay the soles flat on nonstick baking parchment. Using a bone tool, take the toe pieces and hollow out the front into a round shape. Using the tip of a large round icing nozzle, make a hole on either side of the shoe backs. Bend the shoe backs round to curve them. Roll white scraps into a very long, thin sausage of paste for the shoelaces.

Place the royal icing in a small paper piping bag and snip away the end. Pipe a thin line of royal icing round the outline of the sole and stick on the curved toe piece. Wrap the curved back piece around the shoe, sticking it onto the sole. Dab either side of the curved fronts and stick to the toe piece with the shoe tongue in the middle. Repeat to make the other shoe.

Thread the shoelace between the two lace holes and arrange the laces into a bow shape, sticking underneath with royal icing. Leave the shoes to dry and become firm for 24 hours. Avoid moving the shoes or touching them, as they are hollow and very delicate while still wet.

Note: Make the shoes in other colours, such as blue and pink.

The Bear Wedding

Makes bride and groom bears, a pianist bear with a piano, a choirmaster and 3 small chorister bears

150 g/5 oz light brown,
225 g/8 oz black,
125 g/4 oz white and
15 g/¹/₂ oz red modelling paste
(*see* page 24)
cocktail sticks
tube black writing icing
black paste food colouring

To make a big bear, roll 15 g/¹/₂ oz light brown paste into a thick sausage and cut into four for the arms and legs. Roll a 25 g/1 oz oval for the body and a 15 g/¹/₂ oz round for the head; model ears from scraps. Shape the limbs and press in place. Shape the head, secure to the body with a cocktail stick. Press on the ears. Make small black balls for eyes and nose and stick in place. Repeat to make another big bear. Leave both to dry flat on their backs on nonstick baking parchment for 24 hours. Make two medium bears and three small bears using the same method, with 40 g/1¹/₂ oz and 25 g/1 oz light brown paste respectively for each. Dry.

Roll out 125 g/4 oz black paste and cut a piano base and a lid from the template on page 251. Place a thin strip of white paste on the base for the keyboard and paint on black keys. Model three piano legs. Roll a thin black strip of paste, curving it to fit round the sides of the piano. Leave to dry as above. To assemble, pipe black writing icing round the piano base and stick on the side piece. Stick on the legs with a dab of black icing. Paint a cocktail stick black with colouring. Pipe black icing on the long side of the lid and stick in place, then support this with the cocktail stick.

Model the red paste into three books and make white pages from scraps. Model black shorts and white collars, stick onto the three small bears and place the books in their paws. Make black jackets for the two medium bears, place a cocktail stick in one for a baton and stand the other bear behind the piano. Make a black jacket and trousers for one large bear and a white wedding dress and veil for the other. Decorate the dress with white blossoms. **Note:** Remove the cocktail sticks before serving.

Baby Carriage

Makes 1 baby carriage with baby

225 g/8 oz ivory,
25 g/1 oz peach,
10 g/¹/₄ oz black and
25 g/1 oz blue modelling paste
(*see* page 24)
icing sugar, for dusting
¹/₂ batch royal icing
confectioner's glaze

Roll the ivory paste out on a surface dusted with icing sugar. Cut round the templates on page 252 and cut out two sides, one back, one base, one front piece and four wheels. Mark spokes on the wheels, then leave everything to dry flat on nonstick baking parchment for 24 hours.

Model a 15 g/¹/₂ oz peach round for the baby's head and mark on a mouth with a skewer. Model two tiny black dots for eyes and press onto the head. Model two tiny arms with hands and mark details on the hands with a skewer. Leave to dry.

Dab the edges of the carriage pieces with a thin line of royal icing and stick the three base pieces together at an angle. Stick on the side pieces, then stick the wheels onto the sides. Leave to dry for 4 hours.

Model the remaining ivory scraps into a pillow and a blanket. Place the pillow in the pram, then place the baby's head and arms on it. Place the blanket over the baby and tuck the sides in. Roll the blue paste into a thin sausage and shape into a bow. Stick the bow onto the side of the pram. Shape blue scraps into six small balls and flatten out, then press onto the blanket to decorate.

Place the remaining royal icing in a small paper icing bag fitted with a no 2 plain nozzle. Pipe a scroll border round the outside of the pram as shown, and hubs on the wheels. Pipe a loop on the end of the carriage as shown. For a shiny finish, paint with a thin layer of confectioner's glaze.

Graduation Hats

Makes 12 hats

For the cakes:

12 vanilla cupcakes, covered with
piped vanilla buttercream
(*see* page 16)

To decorate:

225 g/8 oz black and 75 g/3 oz
red ready-to-roll sugarpaste
(*see* page 20)
icing sugar, for dusting

Knead the black sugarpaste to soften, then roll out a third on a surface dusted with icing sugar. Cut into 12 small squares, 4 cm/1½ inches wide. Divide the remaining black sugarpaste into 12 pieces. Roll each piece into a ball, then press the top and base to make a flat surface on either side. Pinch round the middle of the cylinder to straighten the sides, making it about 2 cm/¾ inch high. Press a black square onto each base, making sure it is central. Leave the hats to dry on nonstick baking parchment for 4 hours to firm.

When firm enough to handle, roll the red sugarpaste into a thin sausage. Cut into twelve 3 cm/1¼ inch lengths for the tassels. Mark the end of each tassel with a star tool or a small skewer. Lightly dampen the plain end of each tassel with a little cold boiled water and stick onto the centre of the flat top of the mortarboard hat.

Carefully place the hats onto the buttercream-covered cakes just before serving, lifting them into position with a cranked palette knife.

Easter Favourites

**Makes 12 cupcakes with
3 rabbits with carrots,
3 baskets of eggs and
6 decorated eggs**

For the cakes:

12 chocolate cupcakes
covered in vanilla buttercream
(*see* page 16)

To decorate:

350 g/12 oz green,
125 g/4 oz pink,
125 g/4 oz white,
40 g/1½ oz orange,
125 g/4 oz blue,
125 g/4 oz yellow,
50 g/2 oz brown and 15 g/½ oz lilac
ready-to-roll sugarpaste
(*see* page 20)
icing sugar, for dusting
brown food colouring pen
gold edible balls

Roll the green sugarpaste thinly on a surface dusted with icing sugar and cut out 12 discs large enough to cover the cake tops. Stamp each disc with an embossing tool to make a pattern, then press each disc onto the cakes.

To make the rabbit, roll a 15 g/½ oz ball of pink sugarpaste for the body and a 15 g/½ oz white round for the head. Model two pink and white ears and stick to the back of the head with cold boiled water. Roll two small white sausages for the arms and flatten out for the paws, then press in place on the body. Roll two more sausage shapes for the feet and press the ends flat. Press in place on the body. Make a small pink button nose and roll pink scraps thinly for whiskers. Draw on two eyes with the brown pen. Make three rabbits. Model six carrots with orange sugarpaste, using green scraps for tops.

Roll half the blue sugarpaste into three tiny oval eggs. Repeat with half the yellow and the pink sugarpaste. Divide 50 g/2 oz brown sugarpaste into three pieces and roll each piece into two thin sausages. Twist the strands together into a ring to make a basket and position on three cakes. Place a yellow, pink and blue egg in each basket.

Roll the remaining blue and yellow sugarpaste into six larger eggs. Decorate the blue eggs with white and lilac bands and press in gold balls to decorate. Roll small pink and blue balls from scraps and use to decorate the yellow eggs. Place one blue and one yellow egg on each cake.

Pink Blossom Bootee

Makes 1 bootee

225 g/8 oz light pink and
50 g/2 oz dark pink modelling
paste (*see* page 24)
icing sugar, for dusting
$^{1}/_{4}$ batch royal icing (*see* page 26)
rejuvenator spirit or vodka
pearl lustre powder

Roll the light pink paste out on a surface dusted with icing sugar. Trace round the template on page 252 and cut out one sole shape, one toe and side piece, and one ankle strap.

Lay the shoe sole flat on nonstick baking parchment. Using a bone tool, take the toe and side piece and hollow the front into a round shape. Curve the shoe backs round and press the two straight ends together.

Place half the royal icing in a small paper piping bag and snip away the end. Pipe a thin line of royal icing round the outline of the sole and stick the curved toe and side piece onto this. Pipe along the back seam and press together, sticking it onto the sole. Stick the ankle straps round the top with royal icing and fold the two ends over each other. Leave the shoe to dry for 24 hours. Avoid moving the shoe or touching it, as it is hollow and delicate while still wet.

Reroll light pink scraps and stamp out 60 small flowers using a blossom cutter. Roll out the dark pink paste and repeat, making 60 small flowers.

Fill a small paper icing bag fitted with a no 1 plain nozzle and pipe dots in the centres of the light and dark pink flowers. Leave to dry for 2 hours. Mix a little pearl lustre powder with spirit until smooth. Using a tiny amount on a fine paintbrush, dab the centre of each flower to give a pearly finish. Pipe a dab of royal icing underneath each blossom and stick to the bootee, alternating the light and dark pink tones.

Grey Wedding Bears

Makes one bride and one groom bear

275 g/10 oz dark grey,
50 g/2 oz light grey,
25 g/1 oz black,
15 g/¹⁄₂ oz pink and
15 g/¹⁄₂ oz blue modelling
paste (*see* page 24)
cocktail sticks
silver sparkle powder

To make each bear, roll 25 g/1 oz dark grey paste into a thick sausage and cut into four. Roll into two thin arms and two legs with upturned feet. Roll 50 g/2 oz dark grey paste into an oval for the body and 25 g/1 oz into a round for the head; make ears from scraps and press on. Make two bears.

Flatten the body slightly at the base and place on nonstick baking parchment. Bend the arms and legs and stick in place, securing with a halved cocktail stick. Flatten out the head into an oval, then place on a cocktail stick and secure to the body. Using scissors, snip the bears all over, cutting small 'V' shapes into the paste to represent fur.

Roll two small, light grey ovals for muzzles and stick to the bears' faces. Make small black balls for eyes and stick in place. Decorate the ears and feet with small discs of light grey paste and press in place. Mark stitching on the head and muzzle with a quilting tool.

Roll a pink nose from scraps and press onto the muzzle of one bear, then model a small pink flower and press into the bear's ear. Roll a blue nose and press onto the other bear. Model a small black top hat, make a blue hatband and press on, then place over one ear, securing with a halved cocktail stick. Roll black paste into a very thin sausage and cut into short lengths. Press the strips onto the feet and the body to represent stitching as shown. Make a black centre for the pink flower and press in place. Sprinkle the bears lightly with silver sparkle powder.

Note: Remove the cocktail sticks before serving.

New Home

**Makes 1 house with
1 tree and a washing
line with clothes**

20 cm/8 inch square sponge cake
1 batch vanilla buttercream
(*see* page 16)
575 g/1 ¼ lb tan,
175 g/6 oz yellow,
175 g/6 oz brown,
50 g/2 oz red and
25 g/1 oz green
ready-to-roll sugarpaste
(*see* page 20)
icing sugar, for dusting
125 g/4 oz desiccated coconut
leaf-green paste food colouring
green, yellow and brown
writing icing tubes
thick gauge floristry wire

Cut the cake into two pieces lengthways down the middle. Stick one half on top of the other with buttercream to make a tall oblong shape. Cut a triangular piece away from either side of the top of the oblong to make sloping sides to form a roof. Spread the cake with a thin layer of buttercream.

Roll out the tan sugarpaste on a surface dusted with icing sugar. Cut out two oblongs and press onto the sides of the house, then cut two square shapes with a pointed gable for the ends of the house. Press the pieces in place and neaten the corners with a knife to make straight edges. Mark on lines with a knife to represent wood panels. Roll the remaining tan sugarpaste out thickly into two oblongs to cover the roof. Press the oblongs onto the cake, leaving the ends slightly overhanging. Colour the desiccated coconut leaf green with a little paste food colouring. Spread the roof and a 25 cm/10 inch square cake board with buttercream. Scatter the green coconut over the roof and board to cover evenly. Place the house on the green covered board.

Roll yellow sugarpaste out thinly and cut out 10 windows. Lightly dampen the windows with cold boiled water and stick to the house as shown. Roll thin brown strips and stick round the windows for frames, and trim for the roof. Model a small brown chimney and press onto the roof. Roll the red sugarpaste thinly and stamp out 18 blossom flowers. Pipe on stems with the green writing icing, then stick the flowers onto this. Pipe yellow centres into the flowers.

Model a washing line and a tree from wire. Make clothes from scraps and hang on the washing line, fashioning pegs with brown icing. Model small red balls and oval green leaves and press these onto the wire branches.

Smiley Snowman

Makes 12 snowmen

For the cakes:

12 chocolate cupcakes, covered
with white sugarpaste discs
(*see* page 20)

To decorate:

175 g/6 oz white uncoloured
almond paste
700 g/1¹/₂ lb white,
175 g/6 oz red and
50 g/2 oz green
ready-to-roll sugarpaste
icing sugar, for dusting
black food colouring pen
¹/₄ batch blue royal icing
(*see* page 26)

Divide the almond paste into 12 and roll into small, neat balls. Roll half the white sugarpaste out thinly on a surface dusted with icing sugar and cut out discs large enough to cover the balls. Gather the sugarpaste up round each ball to cover it, press the joins neatly together and place underneath, then roll the ball in your palms to smooth. Roll 12 small balls for the heads.

Model two thirds of the red sugarpaste into hats. Roll a flat circle for the brim, then roll a small ball and flatten so that the top is wider than the base. Roll the sides flat, then make a dip in the wider side for the top of the hat. Press the top piece onto the brim and leave on nonstick baking parchment. Roll the remaining red sugarpaste into a thin sausage. Roll a white strand similarly and then roll the two together to make a stripy rope.

Dampen the underside of each body lightly with cold boiled water and stick onto the cakes. Stick on the heads, then the hats. Wrap the red stripy scarves around the necks. Roll green sugarpaste into a large and a smaller green ball and stick onto the front as buttons. Mark two black dots on the head as eyes, attach a scrap of red sugarpaste for a nose and mark on a happy mouth with a skewer.

Place blue royal icing in a small paper bag fitted with a no 0 plain nozzle and pipe snowflake patterns and dots on the cake bases.

Orange Blossom Wedding Couple

Makes a bride and a groom

175 g/6 oz peach,
75 g/3 oz white,
25 g/1 oz yellow,
25 g/1 oz green,
25 g/1 oz orange,
75 g/3 oz black and
15 g/½ oz brown modelling
paste (*see* page 24)
brown food colouring pen
2 plastic cake pop sticks
cornflour, for dusting
sparkle lustre powder

For the bride, mould 25 g/1 oz peach paste into a cone around a cake pop stick, leaving 3 cm/1¼ inches uncovered at each end. Mould the top to make the shoulders and taper the remaining paste inwards to form a waist. Roll 50 g/2 oz white paste into a circle for the skirt. Make a small bodice with white paste and wrap around the top of the bride's body. Roll two thin sausages from peach paste for arms and stick to the shoulders as shown. Press the stick into the cake. Drape the skirt into folds and press onto the body, leaving the folds hanging loosely. Model two tiny white feet and press onto the hem. Mould a 25 g/1 oz peach ball for the head, and place on the stick so that it rests on the shoulders. Press the yellow paste through a garlic press to make the hair and press onto the head, making a curly fringe. Roll the green paste out and cut out small leaves. Roll the orange paste out thinly on a surface dusted with cornflour and stamp out small star-shaped flowers with a cutter. Stick leaves and flowers to the bride's hands and hair with cold boiled water. Dust the bodice and shoes with sparkle powder.

For the groom, mould 50 g/2 oz white paste into a cone around the cake pop stick, leaving 3 cm/1¼ inches exposed at each end. Model two black sausages for arms, and a black jacket. Wrap the jacket round the white shirt. Press the arms onto the jacket. Press the end of the stick into the cake. Roll black paste into two thin sausages for legs and feet and press under the jacket, leaving them hanging over the side of the cake. Model two hands and stick to the arms. Model a white bow tie and stick to the shirt. Mould a 25 g/1 oz peach ball, place on the stick, model ears and press in place. Roll brown paste for hair, cut into a fringe and press in place. Place an orange flower and a leaf on his jacket. Decorate both faces with the brown pen.

Halloween Favourites

Makes 3 ghosts, 3 cats and pumpkins and 3 hats and brooms

For the cakes:

9 vanilla cupcakes decorated with white and green sugarpaste discs (*see* page 20)

To decorate:

50 g/2 oz white,
75 g/3 oz black,
75 g/3 oz orange,
10 g/¹/₄ oz green,
40 g/1¹/₂ oz brown and
10 g/¹/₄ oz light brown
ready-to-roll sugarpaste
icing sugar, for dusting
3 white chocolate malted milk sweets
black food colouring pen

To make the ghosts, divide the white sugarpaste into three 15 g/¹/₂ oz balls, then roll each into a small disc on a surface dusted with icing sugar. Place a white chocolate sweet on three cakes and lift each disc over and smooth down, leaving the edges loosely draped. Draw three black dots for the eyes and mouth on each cake.

To model the witches' hats, divide the black sugarpaste into three 15 g/¹/₂ oz pieces. Roll each piece into a pointed cone, then pinch out the base between your fingers to form a flat edge. Place the hats on nonstick baking parchment. Roll some orange sugarpaste into a thin sausage, flatten out and cut into three lengths, each long enough to fit round the base of each hat. Dampen the underside of each strip with cold boiled water and stick round the hats. Roll out the green sugarpaste thinly and cut into three small squares. Mark the centre of each square and stick onto the hat trim.

Roll out the remaining black sugarpaste thickly and cut out three black cats, following the template on page 253. Roll six white scraps of white sugarpaste and stick on for eyes. Leave to dry flat.

Divide the remaining orange sugarpaste into six pieces. Roll three pieces into rounds, flatten, then mark with a skewer for pumpkins. Roll three brown scraps for stalks and stick in place. Roll the three last pieces into fluted oblongs and mark with a skewer to make the broom. Roll a light brown strip and stick round the base, then roll a brown handle and stick in place. Leave everything to dry for 3 hours. Place everything on the cakes as shown.

Marzipan Fruits

Makes 8 oranges, 4 pears, 4 strawberries and 4 bunches of bananas

125 g/4 oz orange,
125 g/4 oz leaf-green,
125 g/4 oz red,
50 g/2 oz dark green and
125 g/4 oz yellow marzipan
whole cloves
snipped almonds
light brown paste food colouring
granulated sugar

To make the oranges, divide the orange marzipan into eight pieces and roll each piece into a ball. Make an indentation in the top, press a clove into this to represent the stalk. Mark with the tip of a star modelling tool to represent the mottled skin.

To make the pears, divide the leaf-green marzipan into four pieces. Make a ball from one of the pieces, then mould it into a tapered pear shape between your fingertips. Make an indentation in the top and press in a piece of snipped almond for the stalk. Lightly stipple light brown colouring over to represent the skin.

To make the strawberries, divide the red marzipan into four pieces. Roll a piece into a ball, then model into a tapered strawberry shape. Mark with the tip of a small plain nozzle for the skin. Roll the dark green marzipan into four balls and flatten each one. Using a sharp knife, mark into leaves to represent a leafy top and press onto the strawberry. Roll lightly in granulated sugar.

To make the bananas, divide the yellow marzipan into four pieces. Divide each piece into three and roll into small sausages. Pinch the top and base of each to make a tapering shape. Press three bananas together to form a small bunch, then outline the sides of some by painting with light brown colouring. Leave all the fruits to dry on nonstick baking parchment for 1 hour.

Military Wedding Couple

**Makes 1 bride and
1 uniformed groom**

125 g/4 oz black,
125 g/4 oz red,
225 g/8 oz pale pink,
225 g/8 oz white and
25 g/1 oz green modelling
paste (*see* page 24)
3 cake pop sticks
liquid edible gold and silver paint
blue and red food colouring pens
icing sugar, for dusting
edible crystal beads

For the groom, mould two 25 g/1 oz sausages of black paste round two cake pop sticks, leaving the ends exposed. Roll a 50 g/2 oz red oblong for the body. Roll two 25 g/1 oz red arms and press onto the body. Attach two pink hands. Roll a pink 25 g/1 oz ball for the head, cover the top with black paste, then snip with scissors for hair. Model the nose and press in two tiny black discs for eyes, then mark a mouth with a skewer. Place the head on a cocktail stick and place on the body. Press the body onto the legs. Roll black and white scraps and make the collar, epaulettes, belt and cuffs as shown. Roll tiny buttons and belt trim from white paste and paint gold. Make a silver medal and decorate with red and blue pens. Trim the trousers with thin red stripes.

For the bride, mould 50 g/2 oz pink paste into a cone around a cake pop stick, and flatten the top and base; the widest part will form the shoulders. Model a head and features as for the groom. Place the head on the stick. Model two 25 g/1 oz arms with hands and press onto the shoulders. Model a bell shape with 75 g/3 oz white paste and flatten the base. Pinch the top to make a waist, then press the body on the stick into this. Roll 50 g/2 oz white paste out on a surface dusted with icing sugar. Drape the paste over the white bell shape, pleating down the front to form the skirt, fluting out the hem; cut out small squares and place over in layers. Press the remaining 25 g/1 oz white paste onto the bodice and trim across the top. Press black paste through a garlic press to make hair and press round the head. Roll white scraps into a thin veil and press onto the hair. Roll small white and red ribbon roses, make green leaves and press together into a bouquet; secure to the bride with a cocktail stick. Place beads in her hair and on the bodice. Leave the figures to dry flat on baking parchment for 24 hours before standing next to each other, linking arms.

Baby Bear Birthday

**Makes 1 bear with a bottle,
coloured bricks, a blanket
and bootees**

75 g/3 oz light brown,
25 g/1 oz beige,
10 g/¹/₄ oz black,
25 g/1 oz orange,
75 g/3 oz white,
50 g/2 oz green,
75 g/3 oz blue and
25 g/1 oz lemon-yellow
ready-to-roll sugarpaste
(*see* page 20)
cocktail stick
brown food colouring pen

To make the bear, roll 15 g/¹/₂ oz light brown paste into a thick sausage and cut into four. Roll into two arms and two legs. Roll 25 g/1 oz paste into an oval for the body and 15 g/¹/₂ oz into a round for the head; make ears from scraps. Flatten the body slightly at the base, and place on the cake. Shape the arms, making indentations at the end of each with a bone tool, then shape the legs and stick both in place. Flatten out the head slightly, then place on a cocktail stick and secure to the body. Press on the ears. Make a small beige muzzle and mark on dots with a skewer. Roll a small black ball for a nose and press in place. Draw on eyes and brows with the brown pen. Press discs of beige paste on the feet; then, using a skewer, mark these, the arms and head with dots to represent stitching. Mark a belly button. Model a small orange dummy and stick to the face with cold boiled water.

To make the bottle, roll 75 g/3 oz white sugarpaste into a cylinder with one narrow end and make a dip into the thick end to make a bottle shape. Roll 25 g/1 oz green sugarpaste into a strip and teat and press on top, then mark with a knife. Place the bottle on the cake and sit the bear in front of it.

To make the blanket, roll out 50 g/2 oz blue sugarpaste and roll on a pattern with an embossing tool. Stick in place, arranged in folds. Mould the remaining blue sugarpaste into two oblongs. Model the tops and hollow out with a small bone tool, to make bootee shapes. Mark the tops with a crimping tool to make a lacy edge, then roll small scraps for laces and stick on. For the blocks, model the yellow, orange and remaining green sugarpaste into small cubes and mark on letters with an embossing tool. Place next to the bear. **Note:** Remove the cocktail stick before serving.

Stork Baby

Makes a stork and a baby with blanket covering

50 g/2 oz peach,
10 g/¹/₄ oz beige,
10 g/¹/₄ oz lilac,
125 g/4 oz white,
50 g/2 oz orange and
15 g/¹/₂ oz blue ready-to-roll
sugarpaste (*see* page 20)
brown food colouring pen

To make the baby, roll the peach sugarpaste into a smooth sausage with rounded ends. Press in the middle to make a dip, then place the sausage on the cake. Roll a small button nose from scraps and press onto the baby's face. Roll the beige sugarpaste into a small strip and press in place on the forehead to make a curl. Roll the lilac sugarpaste into a large and a smaller ball, then place one on top of the other and press onto the baby's face for the dummy. Mark on eyelids with the brown pen. Roll a small square of white sugarpaste to make a blanket and press a pattern into it with an embossing tool. Drape the blanket loosely over the baby.

To make the stork, roll the remaining white sugarpaste into a cone, then flatten out the base to make a thin edge. Model a thin neck and head with the other end of the cone. Mark the thin lower edge with an embossing tool or skewer to represent feathers, then place the body on the cake. Model two thirds of the orange sugarpaste into two sausages, then model the ends into flat webbed feet and push under the front of the body. Roll the remaining orange sugarpaste into a small cone for the beak and press onto the head. Roll two small discs for eyes and press onto the front of the head. Mark the eyes with the brown pen. Roll a small blue sugarpaste round into a hat and place on the stork's head. Model thin strips of white sugarpaste into the baby's name.

Decorated Christmas Tree

Makes 1 decorated tree

350 g/12 oz ready-to-roll green
sugarpaste (*see* page 20)
900 g/2 lb green, 350 g/12 oz red
and 350 g/12 oz beige
modelling paste (*see* page 24)
icing sugar, for dusting
¹/₄ batch royal icing (*see* page 26)
rejuvenator spirit or vodka
gold lustre powder

Model the green sugarpaste into a cone with a broad base and a pointed tip, about 14 cm/5¹/₂ inches deep. Stand the cone centrally on top of a cake decorated with an embossed gold trim.

Roll the green modelling paste out thinly on a surface dusted with icing sugar. Cut out 80 large and 30 smaller leaf shapes with oval cutters or follow the pattern on page 253 and cut round a template. Keep the shapes covered with clingfilm or in an icing sleeve until needed. Take a leaf shape and press to flick up the outer edge. Dab the thin end with royal icing and stick onto the base of the green cone. Repeat, placing another leaf next to the first. Make a layer all around the base of the tree, then continue to build up another layer on top of the first one. Continue layering until the larger leaves have been used up, then decorate the top of the tree with the smaller leaves in layers, flicking up the ends. As you reach the top of the tree, stick the tips of the leaves to one another to finish.

Roll 60 small red balls and 60 small beige ones. Dab the beige balls with spirit or vodka, then roll in gold lustre powder. Dab each ball with royal icing and stick to the leaves, alternating the colours. Cut out a small star from beige paste, dab with spirit and roll in gold lustre, then stick to the top of the tree with a dab of royal icing. Roll a long thin string of beige paste and wind round the tree.

To make presents, model the remaining red paste into 10 small cubes. Roll beige paste into thin strings and fold over the presents to make looped bows. Place the presents round the base of the tree.

Hobbies & Interests

Anyone would appreciate a cake made specifically for him or her, and this section gives you a variety of projects to make the cake extra special – some small, some a bit more complex! Whether you want to put a Toy Train or a Cinderella Slipper on top, the cake will be remembered as a unique and thoughtful gift. The details you put into the decorations really add value and help to hint at how good the cake will taste!

Pink Cupcakes

Makes 12 pink cupcakes

12 mini Swiss rolls
½ batch vanilla buttercream
(*see* page 16)
350 g/12 oz pink, 350 g/12 oz white
and 75 g/3 oz red ready-to-roll
sugarpaste (*see* page 20)
icing sugar, for dusting
12 glacé cherries

Cut the mini Swiss rolls into 3 cm/1¼ inch lengths and coat with buttercream.

Roll out the pink sugarpaste on a surface lightly dusted with icing sugar and cut into twelve 10 cm/4 inch discs. Place each cake cylinder on a pink disc and bring the sides up. Press the sugarpaste together to enclose the cake, then turn over with the join underneath. Mark lines on the sides with a fine skewer.

Roll the white sugarpaste out into thick sausages and cut into twelve x 16 cm/ 6¼ inch lengths. Roll each piece to make a thin and a thick end, then curl this round and place on top of the pink base.

Roll the red sugarpaste around the cherries to enclose them. Place a cherry on top of each cake to finish.

Blast Off

Makes 1 rocket with launching pad

For the cake:

20 cm/8 inch round cake covered with midnight blue sugarpaste (*see* page 20)

To decorate:

350 g/12 oz yellow, 175 g/6 oz grey, 50 g/2 oz red and 125 g/4 oz blue ready-to-roll sugarpaste icing sugar, for dusting 1 mini Swiss roll 1 tbsp sieved apricot glaze cocktail stick red paste food colouring

Roll the yellow sugarpaste on a surface dusted with icing sugar and cut into 10 thin oblong strips. For the launching pad, roll a small cone of yellow sugarpaste, flatten the top, then mark ridges round the sides with a knife. Place the cone in the centre of the cake, then arrange the strips round it in a circle.

Coat the mini Swiss roll with apricot glaze. Roll out the grey sugarpaste to an oblong large enough to cover the Swiss roll. Place the Swiss roll on the sugarpaste and wrap it up to enclose it. Trim and smooth over, placing the join at the back. Stand the grey body of the rocket upright on the yellow launching pad. Cut out three grey fins and attach these to the base of the rocket, balancing them on the launching pad.

Roll three quarters of the red sugarpaste into a mound shape for the nose cone of the rocket and press in place. Cut out a large and a small red star. Place the small one on the large one and press onto the side of the rocket. Paint a cocktail stick red with a little red colouring and place in the tip of the red nose cone.

Roll out the blue sugarpaste and cut 10 tall triangles. Curve these and leave on a wooden spoon handle covered with clingfilm for 4 hours to harden. Place one curved piece between each of the yellow strips. Decorate the sides of the cake with cut-out yellow stars and a moon shape. **Note:** Remove the cocktail stick before serving.

Camping Trip

Makes a camper in his tent, a dog, fire, a pool with fish, 6 large and 6 small pine trees

For the cake:

25 cm/10 inch and 20 cm/8 inch deep round cakes covered in marbled brown sugarpaste (*see* page 20)

To decorate:

450 g/1 lb green,
225 g/8 oz brown,
175 g/6 oz blue,
75 g/3 oz grey,
50 g/2 oz yellow,
25 g/1 oz white,
125 g/4 oz black and
50 g/2 oz pink ready-to-roll sugarpaste
black food colouring pen
brown and red paste food colourings
1 tiny yellow candle

To make the trees, divide the green sugarpaste into six large and six small pieces and roll each into a thin cone. Using scissors, snip small points all over each to represent the leaves. Roll a small brown trunk for each and press on.

Roll out a thin oval from a quarter of the blue sugarpaste and place on your cake for the pool. Roll small balls from grey paste and arrange round the edge. Model a small yellow teardrop for the fish and make two small flat fins. Press together, then place on the blue water. Make eyes from small balls of white sugarpaste, then mark on black dots. Mark on a mouth with a skewer.

To make the camper and tent, model a triangular wedge from black sugarpaste. Roll out the remaining blue paste thinly and drape over. Cut open at the front and curve back for the tent flaps. Roll 25 g/1 oz pink sugarpaste into a head and two small sausages. Place the head in front of the tent and curve the arms round. Roll a small nose and press on. Mark a mouth and hands with a skewer, roll two small balls of white paste for eyes and press on and mark with the black pen. Flatten a scrap of black sugarpaste for the hair.

Model a dog from a 40 g/1½ oz ball of brown sugarpaste. Roll small balls for legs, strips for ears and a tail and a nose and muzzle for the face and press on. Roll two small white eyes, press on and draw on two black circles. Paint on markings with brown colouring. To make the fire, roll small grey balls and place in a circle. Model logs with brown scraps and place in the fire and round the camp site. Knead red colouring into yellow sugarpaste for a marbled effect, roll into oblongs for flames and place on the logs. Place a tiny yellow candle in the centre.

Designer Handbag

Makes 1 handbag
with appliqué
flower decorations

20 cm/8 inch square sponge cake,
8 cm/3 inches deep
1/2 batch vanilla buttercream
(see page 16)
900 g/2 lb black,
350 g/12 oz turquoise blue and
50 g/2 oz grey ready-to-roll
sugarpaste (see page 20)
icing sugar, for dusting
50 g/2 oz flower paste
(see page 22)
edible liquid silver food colouring
edible glue

Stand the cake upright and cut away two sides at an angle so that the base is wider than the top (see page 250). Leaving the cake upright, spread with buttercream and place on a board. Roll two thirds of the black sugarpaste out on a surface dusted with icing sugar to a square large enough to cover the cake. Lift the sugarpaste over the cake, smooth down the sides and trim the base. Smooth over the shape with a smoother to give a flat finish. Roll the remaining black sugarpaste into a shape for the flap with one straight side and one curved side. Drape over the top of the bag with the straight side at the back of the cake. Mark stitching on the flap with a fine skewer.

Roll 75 g/3 oz turquoise sugarpaste into a thick sausage and mould into the handle. Roll grey sugarpaste into four small studs and two discs for the handle. Leave everything to dry on nonstick baking parchment for 8 hours. Roll 175 g/6 oz turquoise sugarpaste into long, thin sausages. Press the trim onto the sides and base of the bag as shown. Neaten the joins on the corners by smoothing with your fingertips. Roll out the remaining 75 g/3 oz turquoise sugarpaste and, using five-petal cutters, cut out one small, one large and two medium flowers. Cut out two medium black flowers from scraps. Place the large blue flower flat, then stick the medium black flower on this and a smaller blue flower on top. Repeat with the remaining petals, alternating the colours. Place the flowers flat on baking parchment. Roll a small ball of flower paste until soft and press into a silicone mould to make the buttons. Make two round discs with small balls and a larger one with a twisted cord design. Paint the buttons silver and leave on the parchment with the flowers for 8 hours. Using edible glue, stick the small buttons into the flower centres, then stick the flowers and the silver button onto the handbag as shown. Stick on the grey discs, handle and studs to finish.

Cinderella Slipper

Makes 12 cushions with slippers

12 vanilla cupcakes
2 tbsp apricot glaze
575 g/1¼ lb white
and 175 g/6 oz pink
sugarpaste (*see* page 20)
icing sugar, for dusting
edible glue
silver sparkle powder

Trim the cakes flat if they have peaked and brush lightly with apricot glaze. Roll out the white sugarpaste on a surface lightly dusted with icing sugar and cut out 12 discs, 6 cm/2½ inches wide, reserving the scraps. Stick the discs onto the cakes and smooth over lightly. Roll small balls from white sugarpaste and press onto the cake tops.

To make the cushion, model 15 g/½ oz of pink sugarpaste into a small square. Mark with a knife to make indentations for a quilted pattern. Press a small skewer into the sides to make a dotted border and use a small embossing tool to make patterns. Make 12 cushions.

Using the remaining white sugarpaste, model four small tassels for each cushion by rolling a small oblong and marking on lines with a fine skewer. Model a tiny shoe by rolling a small oblong, then hollowing out the centre. Make a small heel and press onto the back. Roll out the remaining white sugarpaste on a surface dusted with icing sugar and stamp out 12 small flowers with a blossom cutter. Roll a tiny ball and press into the centre of the flower.

To finish, stick a cushion onto each cake with edible glue and stick a white tassel on each of the four corners. Stick the slipper on top of the cushion, then stick the flower onto the front of the shoe. Sprinkle silver sparkle dust all over the top of each cake to finish.

Pretty Chic Handbags

Makes 3 designer handbags

450 g/1 lb light green,
450 g/1 lb yellow and
450 g/1 lb pink modelling paste
(*see* page 24)
icing sugar, for dusting
3 round chocolate and marshmallow
cookies, 7.5 cm/3 inches wide
2 tbsp apricot glaze
edible gold, pearl and silver balls
gold and silver liquid edible paint
edible glue

Roll out the green paste thickly on a surface dusted with icing sugar and cut out two 14 cm/5¹/₂ inch wide discs. Brush a cookie with apricot glaze, place a disc either side of it and press all around to enclose. Smooth the edges round to make a flat edge. Press the base of the bag flat so that it will stand up. Smooth all over the round, then make an indented pattern using a quilting tool: mark lines in one direction, then mark in the opposite direction to make small square diamond shapes. Press a gold ball into the centre point of each diamond. Mark round the plain sides of the bag with a skewer for a stitching effect. Roll the remaining green paste into two small balls for the clasp, four small discs 2.5 cm/1 inch wide and two long sausages. Bend the sausages over into handle shapes, then mark with a quilting tool to make stitching. Paint the discs and balls gold and leave everything to dry on nonstick baking parchment for 8 hours.

To make the yellow bag, repeat using the yellow paste. Make the diamond pattern different, marking the lines with the quilting tool in an elongated design so that the diamonds are flatter. Press on pearl balls, paint the discs and clasp balls gold and leave to dry.

To make the pink bag, repeat using the pink paste. Mark the diamonds on with the quilting tool to make them longer and taller. Press on the silver balls, paint the discs and clasp balls silver and leave to dry.

To finish, stand the bags up and, using edible glue, stick on the discs, then stick the handles in place. Stick the clasps on top of each bag.

Tea Pot Time

Makes 1 teapot

For the cake:

10 cm/4 inch square bought
Madeira cake

To decorate:

¼ batch vanilla buttercream
(*see* page 16)
450 g/1 lb blue and
175 g/6 oz white ready-to-roll
sugarpaste (*see* page 20)
icing sugar, for dusting
edible silver balls
¼ batch royal icing (*see* page 26)

Carve the cake square into a ball shape with a sharp knife. Spread the ball with buttercream. Roll out half the blue sugarpaste to a disc large enough to completely enclose the ball and drape the sugarpaste over. Smooth the sugarpaste on and trim neatly. Continue to smooth the ball, then place the cake with the join underneath on nonstick baking parchment. Roll a third of the white sugarpaste into a thin sausage on a surface dusted with icing sugar, then press round the base of the blue ball, smoothing the join together.

Model a small disc from the remaining blue paste for a teapot lid; brush the underside lightly with cold boiled water and stick in place. Mark a dotted pattern on the teapot with the tip of a fine skewer.

Roll thick sausages of blue sugarpaste and model into a handle and teapot spout. Leave these to dry on nonstick baking parchment for 4 hours until firm enough to handle.

Roll the remaining white sugarpaste out thinly and cut out 12 large blossoms and 12 small blossoms using a blossom cutter. Stick half the small blossoms onto the larger ones to make centres. Press silver balls into the centres of all the flowers and leave to dry for 2 hours.

Attach the spout and handle to the teapot with dabs of royal icing. Dab each flower lightly with a little royal icing and place on the teapot, attaching a double one to the top of the lid.

Knitting

**Makes 12 cake coverings,
4 green jumpers, 8 balls
of wool with needles
and 4 strips of knitting
on a needle**

12 vanilla cupcakes
2 tbsp apricot glaze
575 g/1^1/$_4$ lb blue,
175 g/6 oz green,
75 g/3 oz turquoise blue,
50 g/2 oz black and
75 g/3 oz light blue ready-to-roll
sugarpaste (see page 20)
icing sugar, for dusting
edible glue

Trim the cakes flat and brush lightly with apricot glaze. Roll out the blue sugarpaste on a surface dusted with icing sugar and cut out 12 discs, 6 cm/2^1/$_2$ inches wide. Stick the discs onto the cakes and smooth over lightly.

Shape 15 g/^{1}/$_2$ oz green sugarpaste into a 'T' shape for the jumper. Mark on lines with a modelling tool to represent ribbed stitching. Roll thin sausages and press on for a collar and for the base with a trailing end. Make three jumpers and stick onto three cupcakes with edible glue.

To make the balls of wool, roll a small green and a small turquoise blue ball. Roll thin sausages of green and turquoise sugarpaste and wrap round the balls as shown. Roll black sugarpaste round two cocktail sticks for knitting needles. Push into the balls of wool, make two tiny light blue ends and press on. Make three more sets of wool and stick onto cakes with edible glue.

To make the knitting, roll a black sugarpaste sausage for the needle and make a light blue. Roll out a small strip of green sugarpaste, and a thin sausage of green paste. Roll two sausages of light blue sugarpaste. Place the green strip next to a light blue sausage, then a green sausage, then another light blue sausage. Press the pieces together lightly, then mark on lines with a modelling tool to represent stitches. Roll a thin green sausage and cut three short lengths. Stick the knitting on the cupcake, lifting up the centre. Stick the knitting needle at the top of the knitting, then stick the three green strips over the needle for stitches. Repeat for three more cakes.
Note: Warn your guests to remove the cocktail sticks before eating.

Afternoon Tea

Makes 2 large pink serving plates, 6 plain plates, 4 fancy plates, a teapot, milk jug, sugar bowl, cups, cutlery, cheese, cakes and sandwiches

For the cake:

1 x 15 cm/6 inch cake covered in white sugarpaste (see page 20)

To decorate:

250 g g/9 oz light pink,
50 g/2 oz darker pink,
175 g/6 oz white, 50 g/2 oz green,
50 g/2 oz yellow, 15 g/¹/₂ oz deep pink,
15 g/¹/₂ oz lilac, 15 g/¹/₂ oz brown,
15 g/¹/₂ oz dark brown,
25 g/1 oz orange, 15 g/¹/₂ oz blue,
25 g/1 oz peach and 25 g/1 oz light blue ready-to-roll sugarpaste
icing sugar, for dusting
¹/₂ batch royal icing (see page 26)
edible liquid silver paint
red paste food colouring
edible silver balls

Roll 225 g/8 oz light pink sugarpaste out into a thin disc, 20 cm/8 inches wide, and drape over the cake for the tablecloth, fluting out the edges. Roll the darker pink sugarpaste out thinly on a surface dusted with icing sugar and stamp out one 6.5 cm/2¹/₂ inch and one 6 cm/2¹/₃ inch wide discs. Press an embossing tool into the discs and then shape them into serving plates. Place a smaller plate inside the large one and stick onto the centre of the table with a dab of royal icing.

Roll the white sugarpaste out thinly and cut out eight 2 cm/³/₄ inch wide discs for plates. Mark fancy holes in two plates with a skewer. Make four smaller plates, 1.5 cm/⁵/₈ inch wide, and mark fancy holes in two of these. Model a white body for a teapot, sugar bowl, milk jug and teacup. Make a green handle, spout and lid for the teapot and press in place. Make a green handle for the milk jug and press on. Make a yellow handle for the teacup and press on. Make a green lid for the sugar bowl and press on. Arrange the plates and tea set on the table and inside the large pink plates as shown, securing with dabs of royal icing. Use white scraps to model three knives, two forks and two spoons, paint with silver and leave to dry for 2 hours.

Use the yellow paste to model a small cup, two pieces of cheese and three yellow blossom flowers. Stick the blossoms on the teapot and sugar bowl and press a silver ball into each. Model a deep pink and a lilac cake with details as shown and place on the plates. Model small cakes, toast with red colouring and sandwiches as shown and place on plates. Place the cutlery on the table. Place the remaining royal icing in a small bag fitted with a no 0 plain nozzle and pipe a dotted border round the hem of the tablecloth.

Abracadabra

Makes a magician's table with a rabbit in a hat, a deck of cards, a red rose and a magic wand

For the cake:

1 x 20 cm/8 inch round cake
covered in tan sugarpaste
(*see* page 20)

To decorate:

175 g/6 oz claret ready-to-roll
sugarpaste
icing sugar, for dusting
silver sparkle dust
125 g/4 oz black,
50 g/2 oz red,
15 g/¹⁄₂ oz dusty pink,
75 g/3 oz pink,
75 g/3 oz white and
25 g/1 oz green modelling paste
(*see* page 24)
red, black and silver
food colouring pens

Roll out the claret sugarpaste thinly on a surface dusted with icing sugar to a disc 25 cm/10 inches wide. Lift the disc onto the cake and make small pleats in the edge. Scatter silver sparkle dust on the cloth.

Using modelling paste, model a flat black disc for the brim of the hat and a deep round base. Decorate the top of the base with a strip of red paste for the hatband. Roll a small ball of dusty pink paste and press into the centre of the black disc; roll lightly with a small rolling pin to flatten. Roll black paste into a thin sausage for the magic wand. Leave to dry on nonstick baking parchment for 4 hours.

Roll a ball of pink paste for the rabbit's head and press to flatten slightly. Model two small balls for feet, press on and mark with a knife. Roll two small balls for the cheeks and press onto the face. Model two flat ears. Roll a little of the dusty pink paste with the pink paste to make a darker shade, then make inner pieces for the ears and press onto the large ears. Curve the ears over, press onto two halved cocktail sticks and press into the head. Model a dark pink nose and tongue end and press onto the face. Roll two small black eyes and press onto the face. Leave to dry as above.

Roll the white paste out thinly and cut out nine oblongs for cards. Stack five pieces, then leave the other four to dry flat as above. Model a red open rose (*see* page 46) and a green stem and leaf and leave to dry as above. Decorate the cards with the red and black pen and the magic wand with silver lettering. Place the brim on top of the hat, then place the rabbit on this. Arrange the wand, rose and cards on the table.

Treasure Island

Makes an island with an ocean, a beach, an octopus, a shark, a treasure map, palm tree and a treasure chest with gold coins

For the cake:

20 cm/8 inch round cake, standing on a 25 cm/10 inch board, both covered in 700 g/1½ lb light blue sugarpaste (*see page 20*)

To decorate:

225 g/8 oz yellow,
125 g/4 oz pink,
25 g/1 oz grey,
40 g/1½ oz white,
75 g/3 oz brown and
25 g/1 oz green ready-to-roll sugarpaste
icing sugar, for dusting
black food colouring pen
liquid gold food colouring
tube white writing icing

Roll out the yellow sugarpaste on a surface dusted with icing sugar to a half-moon shape. Lift onto half of the cake and stick down with cold boiled water.

Roll 25 g/1 oz of the pink sugarpaste into a ball and place on the board at the base of the cake. Roll pink paste into thin sausages for the tentacles. Make two long tentacles and stick to the base, bend two shorter ones and stick onto the side of the cake. Stick two short pieces on top of the cake, twisting the ends as shown. Model the grey sugarpaste into a triangular shape, then bend the end to make a shark's fin. Stick onto the cake.

Roll out the white sugarpaste into an oblong for the map and curl up the edges with a balling tool. Make snips into the map and stick onto the cake, letting the end curl up as shown. Draw a pattern onto the map with the black pen. Roll yellow scraps into 20 small rounds and flatten them for coins. Paint the coins gold and place on nonstick baking parchment to dry for 2 hours.

Model a third of the brown sugarpaste into a small treasure chest with a base and a lid, then mark with a knife to represent wood. Model the remaining brown sugarpaste into a thick sausage for a curved tree trunk and mark with a knife. Stick both pieces onto the cake as shown. Roll the green sugarpaste out thinly into a strip, make small cuts at intervals to make the leaves, then stick onto the brown tree trunk.

Pipe white lines onto the cake for waves, then stick three gold coins on the map, put some in the treasure chest and scatter the rest on top of the cake.

Circus Fun

Makes 1 circus tent and 1 bear with balloon

75 g/3 oz light blue,
125 g/4 oz yellow,
175 g/6 oz red,
175 g/6 oz lemon,
125 g/4 oz white,
175 g/5 oz turquoise blue,
175 g/6 oz orange,
175 g/6 oz pink and
50 g/2 oz brown ready-to-roll
sugarpaste (*see* page 20)
red paste food colouring
50 g/2 oz tan,
125 g/4 oz white,
15 g/¹/₂ oz light blue,
10 g/¹/₄ oz black,
25 g/1 oz pink,
50 g/2 oz red and
10 g/¹/₄ oz yellow modelling paste
(*see* page 24)
1 x 20 cm/8 in round cake covered
in red ready-to-roll sugarpaste
floristry wires

To make the balloon, roll the light blue sugarpaste into a ball. Paint a cocktail stick red and press into the ball. Make the base for the bear by rolling the tan modelling paste into a small disc. Roll 50 g/2 oz white modelling paste into a ball and place on the disc. Roll 25 g/1 oz white paste into a ball for the head and secure to the body with a cocktail stick. Roll two large balls for feet and two smaller balls for arms and press in place. Flatten two scraps for ears and press in place. Roll two small balls for a muzzle and press onto the head. Roll two small, light blue scraps for eyes, press on two small black balls, then two small white balls. Decorate the feet, hands and ears with pink paste. Make a small pink mouth from a scrap and press under the muzzle. Roll a red ball for the nose and press on top of the muzzle. Roll a small red cone for the hat and press onto the head. Roll a thin red strip, pleat to make a ruffle, then place under the bear's chin. Make a red oval and press onto the tummy. Mark stitching on the tummy, arms and legs with a quilting tool. Roll small coloured balls and decorate the hat, tummy, balloon and base. Press the balloon into the bear's paw and leave to dry on nonstick baking parchment for 8 hours.

To make the tent, model yellow sugarpaste into a square, then pull the top piece up into a point to make a cone. Roll red sugarpaste into thin and thick strips and press on as shown. With one strip, cut a fancy edge with a fluted cutter and press round the top edge of the tent. Roll a small red ball and press on top. Cut a vent into the front red strip, then pull the sides back to represent a tent opening. Decorate the cake with coloured balls and shapes made from the remaining sugarpastes. Bend wires into coils, place coloured sugarpaste balls on them and press into the cake. Make a 'Circus' sign from yellow and brown sugarpaste. **Note:** Remove sticks and wires before serving.

Tutu Time

Makes 12 frilly tutus

For the cakes:

12 cupcakes covered in vanilla buttercream (see page 16)

To decorate:

700 g/1¹/₂ lb pink and 225 g/8 oz ivory ready-to-roll sugarpaste (see page 20)
icing sugar, for dusting
rejuvenator spirit or vodka
pearl lustre powder

Roll out the pink sugarpaste on a surface dusted with icing sugar and cut out 12 discs, 6 cm/2¹/₂ inches wide with a fluted cutter. Cut 12 smaller discs with a 5 cm/2 inch-wide cutter and keep everything covered with clingfilm.

Roll a cocktail stick back and forth around a large disc to make indentations, fluting up the edges. Repeat to make 12 large fluted discs, then place them on the cupcakes. Repeat with the smaller discs and place on top of the large discs on the cupcakes, sticking on with cold boiled water.

Roll the remaining pink sugarpaste into 12 balls. Flatten the base of each, then press the middle to make a narrow waist. Shape the top into two curves to make a heart-shaped bodice. Repeat to make 12 bodice pieces and stick them centrally onto the frilled skirts with cold boiled water.

Roll the ivory paste and press into a small size bead mould. Press on the lid and then tip out the string of beads. Repeat to make about 20 small beads for each cake. Paint the beads with spirit or vodka, then dust with pearl lustre powder. Leave the pearls to dry for 2 hours, then place round the waist part of each tutu. If you don't have a bead mould, roll small balls by hand, then paint them with pearl lustre.

Toy Train

Makes 1 engine, 1 fuel truck and 1 carriage on a railway line

275 g/10 oz grey,
450 g/1 lb dark brown,
450 g/1 lb black,
350 g/12 oz red,
225 g/8 oz yellow,
50 g/2 oz blue and
50 g/2 oz light brown ready-to-roll
sugarpaste (*see page 20*)
icing sugar, for dusting

Roll the grey sugarpaste on a surface dusted with icing sugar and cover a 25 cm/10 inch cake board, then mark on a pattern with an embossing tool. Roll the dark brown sugarpaste out thickly and cut into 30 short lengths to make the railway sleepers. Position the sleepers evenly round the board, sticking on with cold boiled water. Roll half the black sugarpaste into long, thin sausages, then place over the sleepers in two circles for the tracks, and flatten.

For the wheels, roll 25 g/1 oz black sugarpaste and stamp out seven small discs, about 1.5 cm/⁵⁄₈ inch wide. Roll 25 g/1 oz red paste and stamp out seven slightly smaller discs and press them onto the black discs. Roll 15 g/½ oz yellow sugarpaste, cut out eight tiny stars and press seven onto the wheels. For the engine, model a 40 g/1½ oz red oblong of sugarpaste about 8 cm/3 inches long. Roll thin sausages of black sugarpaste and press round the top edge. Dampen three wheels and stick on the side. Roll half the blue sugarpaste into a cube and the remainder into a fat sausage and place both on the base. Make a small black square and place on the cube, then trim the front with black sausages and make two funnels. Roll a red disc and press onto the front of the engine. Cut out some yellow windows and press on.

For the truck, make a 25 g/1 oz red base, with two wheels, about 5 cm/2 inches long. Model a 50 g/2 oz yellow cube, decorate with yellow strips and a blue sugarpaste star and place on the base. Place a black oblong on top of the truck; roll up five logs from the light brown sugarpaste and pile onto the truck. For the carriage, make a 40 g/1½ oz two-wheeled red base as above, about 5 cm/2 inches long. Model a 50 g/2 oz red oblong and a 15 g/½ oz red cube and cover both with a thin layer of black sugarpaste. Arrange as shown with the yellow star. Make two yellow windows and a chimney and stick on.

Dinosaur Dreams

Makes 1 dinosaur on a grassy base

25 g/1 oz light green,
125 g/4 oz purple,
50 g/2 oz yellow,
10 g/¼ oz black and
15 g/½ oz lilac modelling paste
(*see* page 24)
icing sugar, for dusting
cocktail stick
125 g/4 oz bright green sugarpaste
(*see* page 20)

Roll out the light green modelling paste on a surface dusted with icing sugar to a small, thin circle and place on your cake. Take 40 g/1½ oz purple modelling paste and model into a fat teardrop with the widest part at the base. Place on the light green circle. For the head, roll 25 g/1 oz into a small teardrop, make a pointed tip at the front and flatten the back. Roll a small strip of paste out thinly and cut round the edges with the tip of a fluted cutter to make a wavy edge. Press the strip onto the back of the head so that it stands up. Place a cocktail stick into the body and press the head onto this.

Roll a small, thin oval from yellow paste and press onto the front of the dinosaur's tummy. Roll two small yellow ovals and reserve. Roll the remaining yellow paste into two large horns and a small front horn and press onto the head. Roll two small black dots and press onto the head for eyes.

Roll a sausage from the remaining purple modelling paste and cut into four pieces. Model two pieces into back legs, moulding flat feet at the ends and press onto each side of the body, pressing on the yellow ovals. To make the front legs pinch the tops of the sausages to make them thinner, then bend the ends flat and curve them outwards; stick on as shown. Mark on lines with a knife. To make the nails roll the lilac modelling paste thinly and cut into 12 small strips. Model each strip into a long oval shape and press in rows of three onto the front and back legs. Roll the bright green sugarpaste into balls and push through a garlic press to make short green strands. Arrange the strands around the dinosaur for grass.

Note: Remove the cocktail stick before serving.

Garden Friends

Makes a ladybird, a bee, a toadstool, a yellow and red rose on a leafy base

50 g/2 oz green,
50 g/2 oz red,
50 g/2 oz white,
25 g/1 oz black and
50 g/2 oz yellow ready-to-roll
sugarpaste (*see* page 20)
icing sugar, for dusting

Roll out the green sugarpaste on a surface dusted with icing sugar and, using a leaf cutter, cut into four leaves. Mark on veins with a veining tool or a sharp knife. Place the leaves on your cake.

To make the toadstool, roll a small red ball of sugarpaste and flatten slightly. Roll two small balls of white sugarpaste and press together to make a stalk. Press the red top onto the stalk, then decorate the top with small white balls of sugarpaste.

To make the ladybird, roll a small ball of red sugarpaste and flatten into an oval. Cut a ridge down the back of the oval for the wings. Roll a small black round and press on the front for the face, then roll tiny black dots and press onto the body. Roll white balls for eyes and press onto the face, then roll tiny black dots and press onto the white balls.

To make the bee, roll half the yellow sugarpaste into an oblong. Roll black scraps into thin sausages and wrap around the body. Roll two small balls for eyes and press onto the front. Mark on a tiny mouth with the tip of a fine skewer. Roll two tiny balls of white sugarpaste and flatten out. Pinch each wing together to curve up, then press onto the bee's body.

Model a tiny red and a yellow rose (*see* page 46). Arrange the toadstool, ladybird and the bee on the leaves, then place the roses in front of them.

Templates & Guides

On these pages, you will find templates for some of the icing shapes (and one cake shape) as used in this book. Templates such as these are handy if you do not have a selection of metal cutters and don't feel confident drawing freehand. Just trace the pattern you want onto a sheet of clear greaseproof paper or nonstick baking parchment. Roll out the icing thinly, then position the traced pattern over it. Mark over the pattern with the tip of a small, sharp knife or a pin. Remove the paper and cut out the marked-on pattern with a small, sharp knife. Voilà!

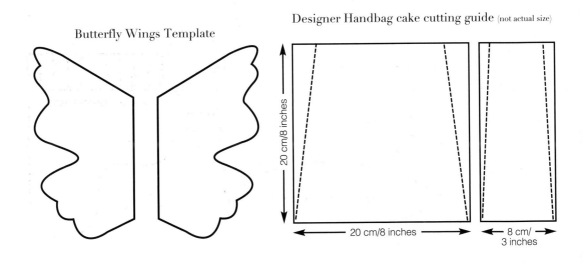

Butterfly Wings Template

Designer Handbag cake cutting guide (not actual size)

20 cm/8 inches

20 cm/8 inches

8 cm/
3 inches

White Bootees Template

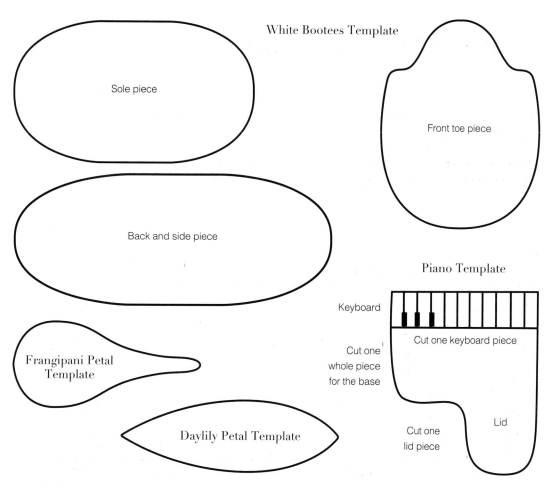

Sole piece

Front toe piece

Back and side piece

Piano Template

Keyboard

Cut one keyboard piece

Frangipani Petal
Template

Cut one
whole piece
for the base

Daylily Petal Template

Cut one
lid piece

Lid

Templates & Guides

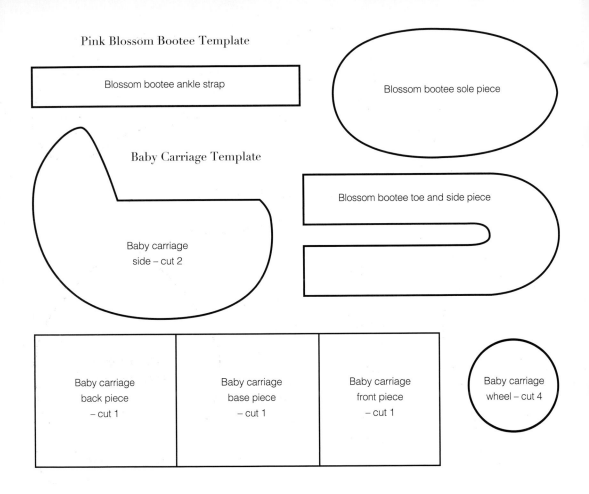

Pink Blossom Bootee Template

Blossom bootee ankle strap

Blossom bootee sole piece

Baby Carriage Template

Blossom bootee toe and side piece

Baby carriage
side – cut 2

Baby carriage
back piece
– cut 1

Baby carriage
base piece
– cut 1

Baby carriage
front piece
– cut 1

Baby carriage
wheel – cut 4

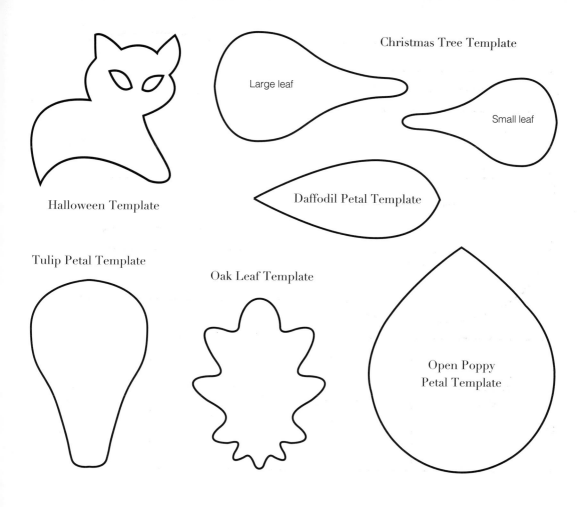

Halloween Template

Large leaf

Christmas Tree Template

Small leaf

Daffodil Petal Template

Tulip Petal Template

Oak Leaf Template

Open Poppy
Petal Template

Templates & Guides

Index

Index